RURAL
MODERN

RURAL
MODERN

Russell Abraham ASMP

images
Publishing

Published in Australia in 2013 by
The Images Publishing Group Pty Ltd
ABN 89 059 734 431
6 Bastow Place, Mulgrave, Victoria 3170, Australia
Tel: +61 3 9561 5544 Fax: +61 3 9561 4860
books@imagespublishing.com
www.imagespublishing.com

National Library of Australia Cataloguing-in-Publication entry

Author:	Abraham, Russell, author.
Title:	Rural modern / by Russell Abraham.
ISBN:	978 1 86470 487 7
Subjects:	Architecture, Modern—21st century.
	Architecture—Environmental aspects.
	Architecture, Domestic.
	Country homes.
Dewey Number:	720.47

Edited by Mandy Herbet

Designed by The Graphic Image Studio Pty Ltd, Mulgrave, Australia
www.tgis.com.au

Pre-publishing services by United Graphic Pte Ltd, Singapore

Printed on 140gsm Gold East Matt Art by 1010 Printing International Limited in China

Contents

Introduction

Russell Abraham

Building technology and architecture are in many ways like fraternal twins. They share the same basic gene pool, but have their own unique appearances and personalities. Just as the lives of fraternal twins are intertwined in curious and sometimes unpredictable ways, building technologies and architecture coexist and interact in a similar fashion. Technology can sometimes leap ahead of architecture and sometimes fall behind. Rarely do they march in step, but they each necessarily affect each other in profound ways giving shape to the architecture we see today.

In the 19th century, rapid advances in materials technology such as the ability to mass produce iron and steel, forced architects to integrate new materials into their designs. Ironically, many new materials and building techniques were used in decorative rather than structural ways. Cast iron was poured into columnar forms and used as appliqué on many commercial buildings. Reinforced concrete, invented in the mid 19th century took almost half a century more before it became a widely used structural material. As factories moved from water power to steam power and eventually electrical power, many things made by hand were now made by machine. The concept of mass production and standardization went beyond consumer goods. The building industry was dramatically affected. By the latter part of the 19th century almost every consumable material in the construction of a house, from wallpaper to roofing tiles, was being produced in a factory or mill. The decorative wooden appliqué designs of the high Victorian era houses were the creation of an automated mill and a new industrial standardization in the building industry that was occurring rapidly in the Western world. The quaint beauty of the San Franciscan Victorian house was the by-product of the imagination of the designer and the accessibility of the factory-created ornamentation.

At the same time that the technology of building was being radically altered by the emerging industrial world, some artists, writers, and architects launched a somewhat backward-looking movement to resurrect the value of handicraft in the arts and architecture. Started in Great Britain by William Morris and John Ruskin, the Arts and Crafts movement spread across Europe and North America in the latter part of the 19th century. It was an attempt to revive both craft and decoration in all facets of design from books, to tableware to architecture. One of the movement's key tenants was an intrinsic appreciation of a material's native qualities. Wood should look like wood, not metal or glass. Pottery should look like the earthen clay that it came from. In architecture, this style translated into sometimes neo-Gothic structures with exposed, unpainted members, and somber hues reflecting a desire to return to the perceived "medieval values" of craft. When the "Arts and Crafts" movement made it across the Atlantic, it had morphed into the "Shingle Style" and quickly became a popular style for the summer homes of the wealthy. McKim, Meade & White would design Neo-Classical banks in Manhattan and "Shingle Style" summer retreats for their owners. It was from these late-19th-century and early-20th-century Arts and Crafts architects that the beginnings of what we know as Modern Architecture emerged.

Modernism, sometimes called the International Style, crashed into the American architectural consciousness right after World War II, even though it had lived in the minds and works of both American and European architects for almost 50 years before. The style had its birthplace in post-World War I Europe, where avant-garde architects and designers from many disciplines sought to create an aesthetic for a new industrial age. The war had ravaged large swaths of Central Europe, offering up a "clean slate" for a new generation of architects who hoped to build a new Europe based on a new social order with new building materials and an entirely new style. Ironically, these progressive architects were inspired by a handful of their American counterparts, such as Frank Lloyd Wright and Irving Gill, whose work they had just begun to see in books. They strongly rejected the eclecticism of the 19th century penchant for the medieval. The mass production of large industrial consumer goods, such as cars, radios, and refrigerators, inspired them to use similar techniques on buildings.

In 1922, a group of influential architects, designers, and painters started the Bauhaus Design School. It was a place where painters, designers, and architects gathered to create a uniform new aesthetic that became the Modern Style we know today. The overreaching philosophy among Bauhaus architects, icluding Walter Gropius and Ludwig Mies van der Rohe, was to develop a building style based on a machine aesthetic. If cars could be created in factories, why not buildings, or at least parts of buildings? The concept of craft—a handmade, unique object—which had been an intrinsic aspect of building going back hundreds of years and a key tenant of the Arts and Crafts movement, took a back seat to the precision of factory-produced materials.

Using newly created machined materials, such as plate glass and mass-produced structural steel, Bauhaus architects created a stark, simple, unadorned architecture of flat roofs, glass walls, and long uninterrupted planes. The ensuing design trope produced an architecture of well-tailored cubes and intersecting planes. In the minds of these Bauhaus architects, there was an essential truth to be found in Euclidean Geometry. The cube became elegant instead of boxy. Repetitive forms became ordered instead of boring. For the most part, ornamentation was eschewed in favor of smooth, white surfaces.

The Bauhaus moved to Berlin in the 1930s but was soon expelled by the emerging Nazi government of Adolf Hitler, who considered Modernism to be too close to Socialism. The school's leading architects were forced to leave Germany and found a friendlier place to hang their hats and their aesthetics in the United States.

Maybe it was inevitable that an architectural style developed for Europe found its strongest adherence in American cities. The country was facing explosive post-war growth and it was boom time throughout most American cities in the 1950s. Pent-up demand for consumer goods of all types spurred spectacular growth and a rapid suburbanization of many American cities. Many urban cores were completely transformed. The eclectic brick and ornamental stone façades of many central cities were rapidly replaced with towers of concrete, steel, and glass with sleek plate-glass storefronts celebrating the new era. Modernism was quickly adopted as the de rigueur design theme in most non-residential building in the post-World War II period.

Starting in the early 20th century, a small but influential group of American architects developed their own style of Modern Architecture. Regional in nature, these individual architects created an aesthetic that grew out of the land rather than placed on the land. They drew their inspiration from the 19th-century Arts and Crafts movement that had been a reaction to the Victorian period's penchant for machine-created ornamentation. Around the United States, architects evolved this "craftsman" style into an indigenous style of their own. In the Midwest, Frank Lloyd Wright created a "prairie school" style he labeled "organic architecture." In California, Bernard Maybeck took the Craftsman Shingle Style to the edge of Modernism. In Los Angeles, Irving Gill pushed the Mission Style to its creative limits. Together, these early-20th-century architects laid the foundations of a new, homegrown, organic architecture. Philosophically, these architects were much more oriented to the building growing out of and being attached to the site rather than being an assemblage of manufactured materials that could be assembled anywhere. The buildings they designed spoke of wood and glass rather than concrete and steel.

While offering a new design paradigm that would transform the urban landscape from New York to New Delhi, Modernism was always a slow burn for residential architects. The sharp edges and simple geometries of Germanic Modernism were always a hard sell to the American design psyche. Without reaching for definitions or labels, in the 1950s and 1960s a group of innovative architects around the United States took Bauhaus Modernism and gave it a softer, more easily accessible vernacular face. They incorporated locally available materials and forms from the simple utilitarian buildings and added Modernist design concepts to create a new strain of Modernism. In the San Francisco Bay Area, architects such as Joseph Esherick, William Turnbull, and Roger Lee created striking houses using locally available redwood and glass. In the American South, Fay Jones and Samuel Mockbee did the same using pine, cypress, and borrowed farmhouse forms. In the Northwest, Jim Olson and Tom Kundig helped create a remarkable Northwest regional style.

Whether we call it Regional Modern, Vernacular Modern, or Rural Modern, it is based on the same principles of creating an "organic" Modern architecture incorporating regional materials and forms. This is something Frank Lloyd Wright talked about nearly a century ago. In the process, siting, weather, and energy conservation and generation came to play an important role. By designing buildings that use less water and little energy, the Rural Modern house helps mitigate the carbon footprint of the construction process. The end result is buildings that are more likely to have shed roofs, large overhangs, and sunshades to mitigate heat gain.

They may have stone or brick walls that function as heat sinks as well as bearing walls. Concrete floors can become passive solar devices, holding heat in winter and cold in summer. Photovoltaic and geothermal heat pumps can be used to reduce energy consumption. Casework is more likely to be constructed of local or sustainable hardwoods than exotic imports from rapidly depleted tropical rainforests. The concept of craft and craftsmanship is reaffirmed and celebrated in all of these houses.

The Rural Modern house is an architectural blend, drawing on both Bauhaus disciplines and American regional architectural sensibilities. A Rural Modern house in California will look different from one in the Southeast or Midwest. Architect Frank Harmon told me that he likes to learn lessons from old buildings, ones built 100 years ago or more. As he says, they "always got it right because they had to. They didn't have the luxury of electricity or air-conditioning." The builders of an earlier time had to be much more concerned about the elements because they had fewer tools with which to control them. Today, many architects are rediscovering these truths, albeit for different reasons. "Green Design" has been a buzzword in architectural communities in the United States and elsewhere for over a decade. The utilitarian buildings of a century ago can offer up forgotten principles of good building design.

This is not to say that Rural Modern is a replication of the past. Rather, historical and regional architecture inform the present and offer inspiration and guidance to contemporary architects. Rural Modern uses the wisdom and intrinsic beauty of the past to create the future. It is an integration of Regionalism, sustainability, and Modernist concepts of openness and livability. It is a revival of an "organic architecture" that Wright championed. In the Rural Modern house the fraternal twins of building technology and architecture can live happily under one roof.

Orinda, California
April 2013

Above: Northern California house, Roger Lee, architect, Roger Sturtevant, photographer from the Roger Sturtevant collection of the Oakland Museum of California.

A New Voice in Southern Modernism

Carter Burton

Page Carter and Jim Burton have been partners since the mid-1990s. They came from different backgrounds—Burton from the Deep South and Carter from Virginia and New England—but they found common

"Simple wooden structures with dramatic stone walls, vertical surfaces wrapped in metal siding, towering colonnades, and walls of glass are all part of their design vocabulary."

ground, both aesthetic and territorial, in rural Virginia where they now practice. Their style of architecture is a distinctive blend of Modernist concepts and Southern architectural themes. As odd as that seems (hold the antebellum columns), their work is as visually stimulating as Richard Miers' or Steven Erhlich's, but with a distinctive regional flavor. Simple wooden structures with dramatic stone walls, vertical surfaces wrapped in metal siding, towering colonnades, and walls of glass are all part of their design vocabulary. Going inside one of their houses is like entering a loft gallery in SoHo in New York or SoMa in San Francisco. Burton likes to think of his residential work as a design laboratory, a place where one can experiment and innovate. He sees his building materials as a painter might see color on his palette. He talks a bit like Louis I. Kahn, who famously said, "What does a brick want to be?" When talking about the steel beams and supports used in one of his houses, he said that the steel needed to express that it was steel. Carter Burton brings a level of creativity and visual excitement in its residential work that is exceptional.

Jim Burton was the son of a high-ranking U.S. military officer whose early years had him moving from base to base, mostly in the southern United States. His father landed an appointment at the Pentagon in Virginia and the family followed. In high school, Burton took classes in architecture and technical drawing and these classes were critiqued by returning students from the prestigious Carnegie Mellon University, giving the sessions an air of authenticity. Burton returned to the South to study architecture at Mississippi State. At the time, M.S.U. had one of the most impressive design faculties in the U.S., while its orientation, led by department chairman Chris Rischer, was to develop a design process that was modern and adaptable to regions, urban or rural. One of the young stars on the faculty was Samuel Mockbee, who would later develop the Rural Studio, a group of students and teachers who design and build projects for the rural poor in the South. It was here at M.S.U. that Burton was introduced to the importance of "defining place."

Page Carter is a native of Virginia, born and raised in Roanoke. She went to the distinguished University of Virginia and majored in art and art history. In her senior year, she took a studio course in architecture and fell in love with the idea of creating buildings. After college, she got a job working for a small architectural firm in Boston. Over the course of a few years, she went from office girl to actually taking on some design responsibilities. She was accepted into the Harvard design program and earned her master's of architecture there. She worked at large firms in Houston and Baltimore on very large commercial projects. Along the way, she got married, had two children, and continued to practice. She and her husband ended up back in Virginia where Carter decided that a smaller, more personal practice suited her just fine. It was here she connected with Burton.

Once out of school, Burton landed a job with a small architectural firm, doing residential design. He eventually designed and built a modern house for himself in rural Virginia near where he worked. He met Carter when she interviewed for a job at his firm and he was impressed with her portfolio that was mostly Modern work in a region where that was unusual. When the time was right, and Carter saw an increased workload, Burton joined her to form a new firm.

Since the late 1990s, the firm of Carter Burton has established a distinctive architectural presence in rural Virginia. Working in a small town, they are necessarily architectural generalists, but their heart is in the residential side of the business. Burton says their work is something of a hybrid of old and new technologies with a focus on sustainability and energy efficiency. He sees a cultural component to being "green", using local materials and local craftsmen in most of his projects. He describes their work as "rooted to a place without being sentimental."

On both the micro and macro level, the architecture of Carter Burton is elegant, regional, and deceptively complex. Working with basic materials and simple programs, they have created some of the most intriguing residential spaces in 21st-century America. Who knew that great American architecture was being created in the rolling hills of the Shenandoah Valley? In their unassuming way, Carter Burton did.

Pond View House

The clients for this house have a deep commitment to art and architecture. Pam Pittinger is an accomplished fine artist and her husband Lynn, a petroleum engineer, is also an accomplished woodworker. They wanted a modern, energy efficient house to replace their 100-year-old drafty farmhouse on their rural property. Located west of Washington, D.C. in beautiful Rappahannock County, the house sits next to a delightful pond, which acts as a catch basin and water supply for the historic farm. Burton's plan for the house was to break it into two halves; a private and a public section. The private contains the bedrooms and roof garden and decks and the public, the primary living spaces. Burton separated each section of the house with a unique exterior treatment, one of darkly stained cedar siding, and the public section with a bright metal cladding that served as both roof and siding. Burton oriented the house so that the primary views from the public section were toward the pond—hence the name, Pond View. The house is integrated into the existing farm structures and becomes part of a compound of old and new buildings. Burton's concept was to strike a tension between the two, but not create aesthetic conflict. The metal-clad portion of the house stands in stark contrast with the weathered barn and outbuildings, and while stepping lightly toward the pond it acts as something of an architectural counterpoint to the somber farm palette of reds and browns. The interiors are also an exercise in contrasts with strong exposed steel structural elements offset with the warmth of hardwood floors and casework fabricated from trees found on the farm itself. Finetuned with energy modeling software, the house's energy bills average US$40 per month.

Carter Burton packs a lot of drama in a simple rural house tucked away in a region not known for dramatic architecture.

Photography by Russell Abraham

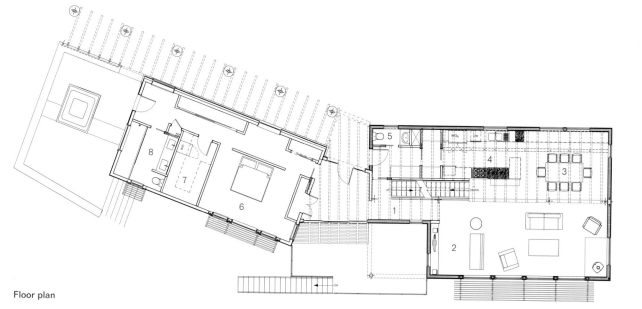

Floor plan

1 Entry
2 Living
3 Dining
4 Kitchen
5 Powder room
6 Master bedroom
7 Walk-in closet
8 Master bathroom

0   12ft

Elk Run Ridge

Driving up to the Elk Run Ridge house in the early evening is quite an experience. The house sits on a ridge line in the middle of 240 acres (97 hectares) of pastureland in the bucolic Shenandoah Valley of western Virginia. With each of its 18 majestic, up-lit, wooden columns circumnavigating its portico, it has the feel of a modern day Monticello.

The house is really two houses under one roof that rakishly breaks about two-thirds through and strikes another pitch-line. There is a large breezeway that separates the building's two parts and gives the arriving guest a dramatic look through to the distant Massanutten Mountains. The house's plan and program is quite simple—a grand room for large family gatherings and a separate studio and guest quarters for extended family visits—but its execution and detailing are innovative and exceptional. The homeowners, Fred and Kathryn Giampietro, wanted a second home to accommodate their large family reunions, but they did not want a national park lodge. They wanted a well-tailored modern house that would fit into the bucolic site—a working ranch that had been part of Kathryn's family for generations. Carter Burton's solution was to give them a box within a box and a third box to house their extended family. The main box is the great hall with its baronial 16-foot high (4.8-meter) fireplace on one end and a very open kitchen and dining area on the other.

The second box has a very cleverly wrapped walnut basket-weave shell that houses the master bathroom, powder room, closets, laundry, and service kitchen. That walnut-clad interior space is then surrounded with an exquisite native stone wall that forms the master bedroom and entry court at the end of the house. As visitors traverse from the great hall to the master suite, they are greeted with the walnut basket-weave wall on one side and the native stone on the other. Burton uses narrow slit windows in the exterior stone wall to paint ribbons of light into the hall and master bedroom while providing privacy. Broad porches that are on both sides of the house are accessed by 9-foot tall (2.7-meter) rollaway glass sliding doors, great for a summer evening party with 200 guests. The grand hall's heroic scale is offset by furniture and casework created in the studio of the renowned woodworkers, George and Mira Nakashima.

Fred Giampietro is a well-known gallery owner and art dealer in Connecticut. He deals in both Americana and contemporary art. He wanted this house to be a statement about both Modernism and vernacular themes. One can only conclude that Carter Burton met his expectations in a grand way.

Photography by Russell Abraham

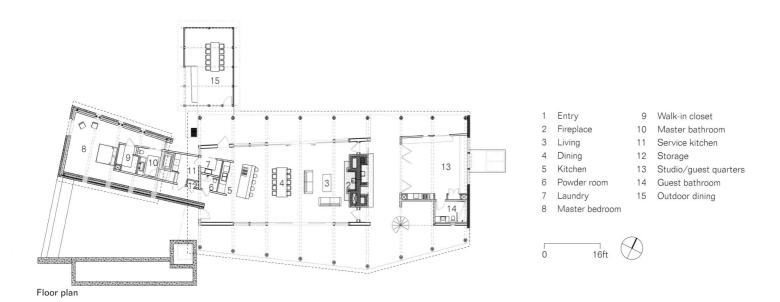

Floor plan

1	Entry	9	Walk-in closet
2	Fireplace	10	Master bathroom
3	Living	11	Service kitchen
4	Dining	12	Storage
5	Kitchen	13	Studio/guest quarters
6	Powder room	14	Guest bathroom
7	Laundry	15	Outdoor dining
8	Master bedroom		

0   16ft

Solar Design with Zen Sensibilities
Chris Larson Architect

Chris Larson is a winsome character who has spent most of his professional life designing houses in the lush Appalachian Mountains of North Carolina. He is a practicing Buddhist who consciously incorporates its values and perceptions into each of his projects. He is also a graduate of MIT and a very astute 21st-century architect, incorporating the latest advances in materials and technology in crafting his projects. His work exemplifies a respect for regional identities, a strong grounding in sustainable technologies and a hard-to-define architectural élan that

was the family business. He completed his undergraduate work at the University of Utah where he majored in computer science. After college, he moved to Boston and attended the Boston Architectural Center. From there it was a short subway ride across the Charles River to MIT where he earned his master's degree. At MIT, Larson was influenced by Maurice K. Smith, who was a disciple of Wright and espoused an organic and regional Modernism. Having a strong affinity for the out doors, a friend invited Larson to spend a summer in the Blue Ridge Mountains as a river guide for a rafting company. Larson jumped at the opportunity and soon found himself designing resort and recreational facilities for the rafting company in the off-season. He developed an affection for the region and stayed setting up a practice in

"His regionalist approach to architecture allows him to create sophisticated buildings that both make unique architectural statements and fit into the environment in a satisfying way."

makes it both interesting and appealing. Larson has been practicing in Asheville, North Carolina almost his entire professional career. His clients are a steady stream of people wanting to build a family or retirement home in the beautiful Blue Ridge Mountains that border the western side of the state. He has reworked the mountain cabin trope and given it a strong dose of Modernism without it looking like a Long Island estate. His regionalist approach to architecture allows him to create sophisticated buildings that both make unique architectural statements and fit into the environment in a satisfying way.

It seems that Chris Larson was destined to be an architect from the beginning, although he may not have known it. His father was the founding partner of a large architectural firm in Omaha, Nebraska. Larson grew up around the profession and even worked in his father's office for summer employment in college. Larson jokes that he went into architecture because he didn't know what else to do with himself and it

Asheville initially, a sleepy village, but now a vibrant regional resort. He says that many of his clients come to him with a great respect and appreciation for the natural beauty of the area and want to take the time to build their ultimate house.

Larson has maintained his one-person practice since he began— he prefers it that way. The smallness of his firm allows him to give his undivided attention to each of his projects. His buildings are meticulously detailed, down to the interior finishes and fixtures. Larson has even developed a line of furniture made by local craftsman from regional hardwoods. He says that he likes to reach back to the world of nature to find patterns and inspiration for his architecture. In some intangible ways, his buildings evoke a Buddhist sense of serenity and oneness with nature. Larson's houses make an aesthetic arch from Eastern thought to Western design without being kitsch or quaint. It takes a rare talent indeed to pull that off.

Knoll House

With its deep eaves and soaring rooflines, the Knoll House looks like another butterfly house, but it's more than that. This house is a well-conceived passive solar designed house whose roof angles, eaves, and window patterns are carefully calculated to capture solar heat in the winter and cooling in the summer. Larson believes it is important to give owners a sky view from some windows in each of his houses and the Knoll House, with its dramatic clerestory windows, certainly does that. The main public spaces face south and catch wooded views and winter warmth from the "solar aperture" Larson has created. A large masonry wall with a broad arch separates the two sides of the house and also serves as a heat sink in Larson's passive solar design. The interiors are finished with native poplar and yellow pine, much of it milled from trees on the site.

The Knoll House stands as strong witness to the argument that green building does not have to be boring building.

Photography by David Dietrich

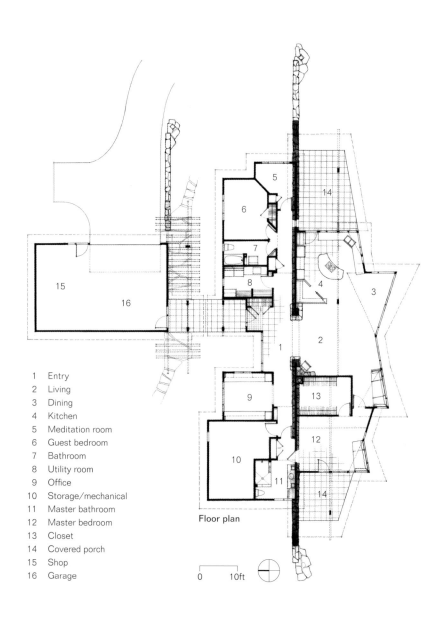

1 Entry
2 Living
3 Dining
4 Kitchen
5 Meditation room
6 Guest bedroom
7 Bathroom
8 Utility room
9 Office
10 Storage/mechanical
11 Master bathroom
12 Master bedroom
13 Closet
14 Covered porch
15 Shop
16 Garage

Floor plan

0   10ft

Creating Sustainable Architecture

Daniel G. Smith & Associates

Alternative building methods and energy conservation get a lot of press these days, but few architects actually use these techniques to build anything noteworthy. Daniel Smith of Berkeley, California is one who has been incorporating green building methods since he started his practice over 30 years ago.

Smith still creates conventionally framed residences and commercial buildings, but his firm has achieved cutting-edge advances into alternative building methods, using everything from straw-bales to

"Smith's architecture is simple and clean, a bit eclectic, but always cutting edge in its environmental saneness."

prefab, from lime or earth plasters to SIP panels. He has successfully used straw-bale construction to create high-end residences as well as modest farm working housing, realizing some 50 straw-bale structures in the United States and abroad, serving a variety of functions. Smith's firm, DSA Architects, has completed several LEED Gold and Platinum projects and received AIA awards for their work, among them a dining hall and a prefab net-zero townhouse in Oakland, California.

Working with his long-time associate, Dietmar Lorenz, and trained in the green Modernist German tradition, they have become one of the pioneering firms in the U.S. for alternative material construction and energy efficient design. Lorenz describes straw-bale construction as the ultimate carbon sequestration technique, since farmers used to burn their leftover straw, releasing excessive CO_2 into the atmosphere. Instead, turned into highly insulating walls, the straw isolates enough carbon to offset the embodied energy of the other building materials, ending up with carbon neutral construction or even a carbon sink. And, of course, straw is not grown for houses, but an agricultural waste product of food production, abundant and annually renewable. Yet the biggest benefit of straw-bale construction or other energy and resource efficient materials

and methods is the drastic reduction in the ongoing energy use and operating cost. Being far more efficient than standard construction, this next generation of passive solar design needs only a modest photovoltaic system to produce as much or more power than it consumes.

The firm's competence in structural design has come into play in consulting and designing housing for developing world countries that is livable, economical, and safe. Traditional masonry houses in many areas risk deadly collapse in earthquakes. Smith has been involved in designing alternative low-cost housing systems in Mongolia, and lending his expertise on rebuilding projects in Pakistan and Haiti after devastating earthquakes. DSA has consulted and designed safe and economical structures using alternative concrete block, straw-bale construction, and other potential building materials.

Smith grew up in Washington, DC where his father was an administrator for a national higher educational organization. He was always fascinated with design and structure and thought he would eventually end up as a car designer, but four years at Yale with a major in architectural history shifted his thinking. The renowned architectural historian, Spiro Kostof, persuaded Smith to follow him from Yale to the University of California at Berkeley where he earned his master's in architecture. It was here he met the influential architects, Sym Van der Ryn and Sanford Hirschen, who were at the forefront of the environmental design movement in architecture. Smith's first house was a prefab affair that he designed and built for his sister in upstate New York. After working for Hirschen for a few years, he wanted more hands-on experience and he created his own design/build/develop business for a few years before starting his own architectural firm. One of his early architecture projects was a temple for the large Sikh community in the San Francisco Bay Area. Incorporating solar features into homes and townhouses, he began to steadily add the concepts of alternative building techniques and energy conservation into his work.

Smith's architecture is simple and clean, a bit eclectic, but always cutting edge in its environmental saneness. He allows the environmental demands of the building to play an active role in its design and express its green features in many ways. Rather than hiding the photovoltaics, they become part of the design, and that passive strategies should drive the design. For instance, he contends that rather than over-glazing a west façade (and hiding a huge, power-hungry air conditioning unit behind the house), a smart fenestration design with additional shading elements as part of the façade will go a long way to control solar heat gain. He talks about his hybrid electric car and admires how the designers built the car around the concept of its power plant. The Louis Sullivan dictum "form follows function" comes to mind. DSA Architects has designed and built four net-zero energy houses and keeps track of their performance, and is currently working with a developer to incorporate these concepts in a larger, multi-family scale project of 30 units. While the built environment produces half of the CO_2 emissions, and architects may or may not save the planet, at least the innovative work done by architects such as Smith will go a long way toward helping make it a more livable place.

Sonoma Family Farmhouse

DSA Architects designed the Sonoma Family Farmhouse for a San Francisco-based family who wanted a deep green building for their bucolic site and organic farm in the heart of California's historic wine producing region. Using the vernacular farmhouses and aging chicken coops of the surrounding farm community for design archetypes, they created a collection of simple gable volumes linked by an undulating, living roof-covered walkway as the path from the creek traverses through the house and pool area and up to the pond.

The main house is 4,000 square feet (371 square meters) of mostly straw-bale construction signified by 24-inch (61-centimeter) thick plastered walls and contrasted by a metal-sided garage wing. Dietmar Lorenz describes it as "passive solar design with a microchip," referring to the fine-tuned interaction of active and passive solar design elements with "smart house" controls. DSA used a solar-thermal system to heat the pool and domestic hot water and then developed a subterranean sand bed heat sink that would hold the heat for several weeks at a time for space heating. Backup and radiant cooling can be provided by a ground-source heat pump, although the house is designed to stay cool with natural ventilation. With the bulk of the hot water and space conditioning needs covered by solar systems and other passive means, the energy output of the photovoltaic system is expected to exceed the demand of the house, adding renewable power to the grid.

Water conservation was another important goal. An old swimming pool was covered and converted into a rainwater cistern, which provides much of the water for toilet flushing and irrigation for the living roofs and drought-resistant landscaping. This is also complemented by a gray water system. Building materials were selected based on sustainable and healthy building criteria, and are as locally sourced as possible. The wood is FSC certified, concrete has high-fly ash content, and insulation almost entirely cellulose or mineral-based. While some of these "green" attributes remain visible, such as well-integrated solar systems, all blend into an unpretentious architecture that celebrates the spaces created, how the light travels through a room, how indoors and outdoors connect, creating comfortable spaces for people.

Working with consultants Sherwood Design Engineers, Tipping & Mar, Timmons Design Engineers, Sentient Landscape, and Navarra Interior Design, and with Hammond Fine Homes as the general contractor, the project is slated for LEED platinum certification.

Photography by Russell Abraham

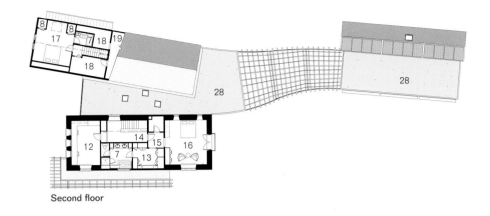

Second floor

First floor

1	Entry
2	Living
3	Dining
4	Kitchen
5	Pantry
6	Family room
7	Bathroom
8	Closet
9	Bedroom
10	Powder room
11	Broom closet
12	Study
13	Dressing room
14	Gallery
15	Vestibule
16	Master bedroom
17	Guest bedroom
18	Storage
19	Attic
20	Changing room
21	Mechanical
22	Bar
23	Outdoor living
24	Outdoor kitchen
25	Trellis
26	Loggia
27	Recycling
28	Living roof
29	Garage

0   25ft

Architectural Polymath

David Stark Wilson

Some people consider Northern California the most livable part of North America. Its rolling coastal hills are graced with vineyards and orchards. The magnificent Sierra Nevada mountain range is covered in snow six months of the year and offers a ready playground to skiers and hikers alike. It is the kind of place where a person can get around for nine months of the year in shorts, sandals, and a sweatshirt and many people do. It is also the home of Intel, Apple, Google, and Facebook. The great inventors and entrepreneurs of the 20th-century's post-industrial society have chosen to make Northern California their home. It is a place where great ideas can be nurtured and grown; a place where intellectual curiosity, entrepreneurship, and an outdoor-oriented lifestyle blend together in an almost seamless fashion.

It is here that David Stark Wilson was born and raised and established himself as an architect. He is a polymath in an environment where being a polymath is not that unusual. Wilson is a man of many talents, endless curiosity, enormous intellect, and a good eye for well-crafted

> *"Not only designing a building for his clients, Wilson is thinking generationally to the building's next inhabitants."*

architecture. His hands-on approach to architecture is both practical and sublime. He has learned how to practice a complex art with a rich history outside academia by seeing, doing, and constantly striving.

Wilson was a typical child growing up in Berkeley, California in the 1970s. His father was a computer scientist who found solace in the great outdoors—a fun family weekend would be scaling some mountain in the nearby Sierras. Wilson believes that he and his sister—at nine and six respectively—were the youngest people ever to climb Mt. Shasta. At an elevation of 14,161 feet (4,316 meters), Shasta is one of the tallest mountains in North America. Mountaineering would continue to be a significant avocation for Wilson.

Wilson initially majored in mathematics at the University of California, Berkeley. He has always set a high bar for himself and academia was no different. At Berkeley he soon realized that there were mathematical minds with much sharper pencils than his. The physical world had always held an interest for Wilson and Venn diagrams and Euclidian forms translated easily into Japanese cabinetry and design. In an effort to earn money for school, Wilson started doing small construction jobs for his neighbors in Berkeley. These neighborhoods were dotted with houses designed by the great Beaux-Arts architects, Bernard Maybeck and Julia Morgan. The Bay Area Shingle Style architecture, which they and their counterparts developed in the early 20th century, has endured to the present day.

By the end of his senior year at Berkeley, Wilson sensed a major career change was in order. His small remodeling projects in school gave way to larger building projects. He became a design-build architect in short order and his first major commission was a house for his mother. He designed and built the house with the help of his sister and a few friends from high school. Doing most of the construction themselves from foundations to casework, Wilson says, "We salvaged granite from a quarry in the Sierra foothills and cut it on site, flaming pieces with a torch to roughen them. The granite, Douglas fir, and hand-applied white gypsum plaster became the palette of materials for the home."

Stylistically, Wilson started from the beautiful Arts and Crafts houses with which he was most familiar. He instinctively appreciated their fine proportions and attention to detail—the Maybeck homes are sometimes compared to Japanese cabinetry with their intricate wood detailing. But he was also aware that he lived in 21st century not the early 20th, so he did his homework. He observed the work of contemporary architects who integrated traditional forms with modern design ideas. At the national level, Will Bruder and Antoine Predock were iconoclastic architects

experimenting in ways that were creative and innovative. Locally, Richard Fernau and Stanley Saitowitz were young Bay Area architects whose distinctive regional modernism Wilson looked to for inspiration and ideas. As he says, "While reinventing the wheel on each project is important, at the end of the day, the wheel still has to turn."

Since his early Berkeley houses, Wilson has developed a distinctive architectural style that incorporates both Modernism and traditional forms. In much the same way that Samuel Mockbee was an innovative regional modernist in the South, Wilson carries that torch in Northern California. He borrows forms from the utilitarian structures he found in the Central Valley as Mockbee did in the rural South. He consciously uses the ever-present nature of Northern California from the rolling hills of the Coastal Range to the rocky faces of the Sierra Nevada to shape and color his ideas. He takes the best ideas of the Arts and Crafts architects and works them into his designs in new ways: using Maybeck's oversized clerestory windows and stretching them; or taking a simple shed roof, inverting it and making it into a bay. Maybeck's deep eaves are now stretched even deeper and supported by tall thin steel columns usually painted bright red. The clever, articulated staircases Maybeck did in wood, Wilson does in stainless steel.

All of Wilson's work has a strong attachment to both nature and the land that it sits on. He likes to think of his architecture as being part of the land and not on top of it. For this reason, natural artifacts are often built around rather than over and the colors of surrounding hillsides or woodlands find their way into finishes and textures. Woods, metals, and stones are left unfinished or rough. One of his favorite building materials is Cor-ten steel, a naturally rusting steel with an intense color. Wilson says, "The colors in nature resonate for all of us, yet there is a general reluctance to introduce color into architecture. Color is used in our projects to emphasize elements of the architecture and also to connect to nature." Not only designing a building for his clients, Wilson is thinking generationally to the building's next inhabitants.

Through observation, discipline and a hands-on approach to design, David Stark Wilson has created a unique regional modern style of architecture that both pays respect to his antecedents and shows us a way into the future. It is an architecture that is energy conscious, people friendly and strikingly beautiful. His buildings sit on the land in rational fashion and grace the environment. He has reinvented the wheel and the wheel not only still turns, it glides.

Tahoe Ridge House

Straddling California and Nevada, Lake Tahoe is considered by some to be one of the great wonders of the natural world. It is the largest alpine lake in North America and the second deepest. At 6,220 feet (1,895 meters) above sea level, its water clarity is legendary. Although known as an international resort and venue for the 1960 Winter Olympics, building at the lake has become highly restricted in recent years.

This was Wilson's second home for this client, a professional couple from the San Francisco Bay Area, who wanted a mountain home in the Sierras. The Tahoe Ridge House is located on one of the last large, buildable parcels in the Tahoe area. Eight acres (3 hectares) of land with dense stands of white and red fir slope upward to the rocky granite ridge crest that becomes a backdrop to this exceptional site. A large male black bear has lived in the boulders above the house for many years and remains undaunted by recent construction, occasionally strolling unhurriedly down the new entry drive.

The home's design was inspired by the vernacular mining and stamp mill buildings in the Tahoe area. Long before Tahoe was a ski resort, it was a Gold Rush destination. The stamp mills were used to pulverize hard rock into fine silt from which the gold could be removed. All movement of material within the mill was achieved by gravity and hence the structures are characteristically elongated vertically.

Significant mountain vistas were a key design consideration for Wilson with views of the mountains of Nevada to the north and to Tinker's Knob and the Sierra Crest to the south needing to be seen. This resulted in a floor plan that sprawls via two orthogonal axes and ascends vertically to the north to the study and master bedroom. The experience of flow along the axes is enhanced by a clear rhythm of 10-inch-by-10-inch (25-centimeter-by-25-centimeter) recycled Douglas fir structural posts that tie in with the roof framing above.

Wilson used a mix of recycled cedar and Galvalume metal siding applied as a tight skin to pay further homage to the old mining buildings. On the interiors, Wilson used large recycled timbers and heavy metal bracketing that both continue the 19th-century industrial aesthetic and functionally support the substantial snow loads of winter. Large Sierra White granite blocks were cut and shaped to form the fireplace hearths. Wilson's Tahoe Ridge House is clearly rooted in and derived from its mountainous site.

Photography by David Wilson

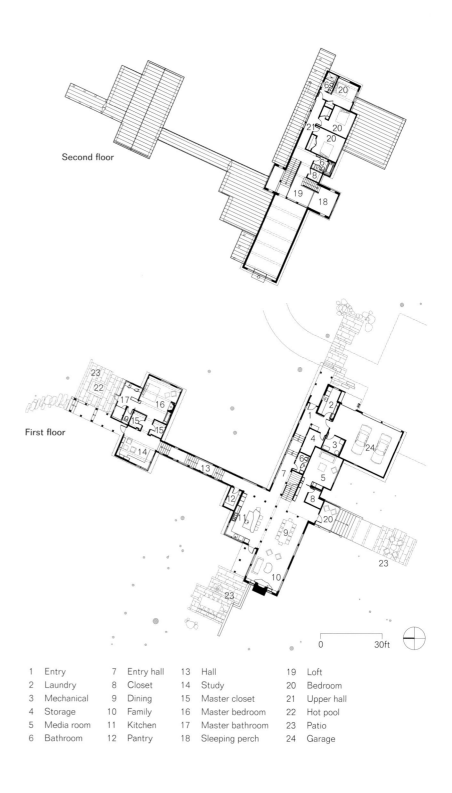

Second floor

First floor

1	Entry	7	Entry hall	13	Hall	19	Loft
2	Laundry	8	Closet	14	Study	20	Bedroom
3	Mechanical	9	Dining	15	Master closet	21	Upper hall
4	Storage	10	Family	16	Master bedroom	22	Hot pool
5	Media room	11	Kitchen	17	Master bathroom	23	Patio
6	Bathroom	12	Pantry	18	Sleeping perch	24	Garage

An Eponymous Practice
Distinctive Architecture

Bill Waddell is the sole practitioner of Distinctive Architecture, a small, residentially oriented office in Durham, North Carolina. His mild manner and Southern accent belie his passion for

"Waddell is neither a Classicist nor Modernist—each house he creates is designed around his client's needs and tastes."

architecture and masterful command of his art. Living in a more conservative region of the United States, his work is anything but conservative. It represents a Regional Modernism adapted to the unique and beautiful environment of the American Southeast and his work is inspired by the great early 20th-century Modernists Frank Lloyd Wright and Harwell Hamilton Harris. It takes popular Modernist themes and gives them a striking regional twist, resulting in designs that are simple, refreshing, and elegant.

Waddell had architecture in his blood from a very young age. His parents hired an architect to draw the plans for their home when he was very young and as a schoolboy, he would pull the original plans out of a bedroom closet and spend hours studying them. Luckily, one of the better architecture schools in the country was just down the road at North Carolina State and its small program with an outstanding faculty gave the young Waddell a chance to study with some of the most famous architects of the time. He took a year off, worked for a firm, and then returned to school to complete his professional degree. His year off gave him time to learn how the design profession functions and renewed his love of architecture.

Just out of school, he worked for a mid-sized firm in Chapel Hill that struggled financially, but gave young architects a high level of responsibility. The principals mentored their young architects instead of dictating their own concepts and Waddell soon found himself the lead architect on large commercial projects. With this rich, hands-on

experience, he easily passed the state licensing exam and now found himself in a position to "hang his own shingle." Teaming up with an old friend who had a contracting business, they formed a design-build firm that specialized in custom home design and construction, designing modern houses and building them efficiently for individual clients. Along the way, Waddell's friend realized that they could control costs and improve efficiency if they had a software program that would control construction scheduling. Working with his friend's brother, they built a construction management software application to run their company's business. It was a Windows-based system that had exceptional updating abilities and ease of use. In a matter of a few years, Waddell went from being an architect to a software developer. The software company began buying up all their competitors and at its zenith, their combined construction management software was being used to manage the construction of nearly half the homes built in the U.S. Waddell found himself an executive within a software firm with over 1000 employees. In something of a "rags to riches to rags" scenario, the company had taken on a large debt load to facilitate expansion of an internet-based solution to knit the fragmented building industry together, and was just about to "go public" when the internet bubble burst in the spring of 2000. The company was wiped out. After some thought, Waddell decided it was time to return to his professional roots and restart his practice.

Waddell sees his years in the software industry as an essential learning experience, finding the disciplines from software development can easily transfer over to architecture. He mentions how Christopher Alexander's book, *A Pattern Language*, is used today as a textbook for software engineers. He says that there is a process-driven analysis that works for both software development and architecture. He likes to talk about an 80/20 rule, where you can get 80 percent of what you want with

100 percent of your budget. To get 90 percent, your costs will double. To get 95 percent, they will double again. He advises his clients to stop at a reasonable place; somewhere less than the asymptotic 100 percent.

Waddell's clients tend to come to him after they have exhausted their search in plan books and on the internet and want a house that says something truly unique about them, and he spends a long time working with them to develop their ideas and articulate their desires. Being a native son, he develops designs that work well in North Carolina's temperate climate. Waddell is neither a Classicist nor Modernist—each house he creates is designed around his client's needs and tastes. But underneath the veneer is well-thought-out architecture that is informed by both Modernist principles and regional tastes and needs. His firm name, Distinctive Architecture, may, after all, be eponymous.

Three Pavilions

The Three Pavilions is quite remarkable on a number of levels. Tucked away on a difficult lot in an upscale subdivision of Durham, North Carolina, its sage green exterior and inverted gabled roof dramatically set it apart from its neighbors. But there is more here than shock value. The house provides the homeowners with the comfortable ecological lifestyle they were seeking while providing workspace for their individual avocations. She is a retired dentist who creates fashion jewelry and he is a retired physician who creates large-scale metal sculpture, all in a neatly contained workshop in one of the pavilions.

Because of a creek and small flood plain adjacent to it, the property itself presented a major design challenge. An overflow basin had to be provided to regulate storm water before it reached the creek. Waddell's solution was to divide the house into three distinct units and place it on the upper rear part of the lot. He then designed the overflow basin for the lower section and several man-made bogs that naturally filter the stormwater before it enters the creek. By controlling stormwater and containing runoff for later landscaping use, a major drainage problem was solved.

The pavilions are arranged around a gravel courtyard that can serve a variety of functions, from summer patio to car parking. Its permeable surface allows water to flow naturally to the bog gardens before excess water heads on to the overflow basin and, finally, to the creek. The main pavilion has a sweeping roof line with large west-facing windows that bring in copious sunlight limited only by deep eaves and a series of roll-down shades. On the north side of the great room, Waddell placed a three-season screen porch complete with fireplace. This indoor–outdoor space smoothly integrates into the living and dining rooms and is ideal for summer gatherings. The great room is decked out in lively colors and filled with the artwork of both owners.

The master suite pavilion is connected by a short bridge, which also becomes an art gallery and storage area. The master suite is a repetition of the design with gorgeous views of the property's natural woodlands. The pavilion that faces the street functions as the couple's workshop and is filled with welding and jewelry-making gear. This pavilion acts as a buffer to the suburban street and establishes a distinctive architectural presence to the neighborhood.

Photography by Russell Abraham

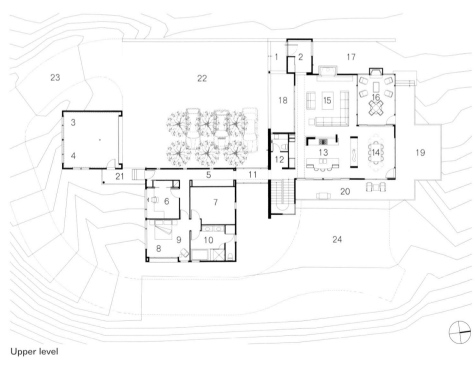

1   Entry porch
2   Main entry
3   Studio
4   Future bathroom
5   Gallery
6   Office
7   Closet
8   Master bedroom
9   Reading nook
10   Master bathroom
11   Bridge
12   Powder room
13   Kitchen
14   Dining
15   Living
16   Screened porch
17   Garden
18   Koi pond
19   Deck
20   Grillmaster's deck
21   Porch
22   Upper auto court
23   Upper driveway
24   Lower auto court

Upper level

Deck House Re-do

In the 1950s and 1960s in the United States there were a series of kit home manufacturers that sprung up. These manufacturers offered predesigned homes with precut lumber and finishes, ready for a construction crew to quickly erect on a pre-laid foundation. Deck House was one of those manufacturers. Their signature design feature was a manufactured cedar roofing system that simplified roof design and gave the houses an attractive, exposed tongue-and-groove wood ceiling. There were a handful of these building manufacturing companies that endeavored to integrate modern design, industrial manufacturing techniques, and the demand for efficient, easily constructed houses.

The owners of this Deck House loved the warmth of the original cedar ceiling, but felt a need to rework the floor plan to fit their family's needs. They also had an appreciation for Mid-Century Modern design and wanted Waddell to be faithful in spirit to the house's original design intents.

Waddell's solution involved removing a number of walls that separated the kitchen, dining, and living areas into strongly distinct spaces so the post-and-beam structure could be properly expressed and the family areas could be used as one large gathering space defined by cabinetry and furniture, rather than walls. Horizontal window bands were replaced with floor-to-ceiling glazing to further reinforce the structure and provide a stronger connection to outdoor views and living areas.

The house is long and narrow with the garage and short dimension of the home near the street. The original entry foyer was in the middle of the long side of the home, requiring guests to walk along the face of the house a good distance before arriving at a combined entry/formal dining room. Waddell changed this by re-purposing and enhancing an existing storage corner in the garage into a new, dramatic entry foyer directly adjacent to the parking area. This space provided a natural circulation route from the existing garage, through a new family entry/mudroom, into the foyer and on to the kitchen.

Several rooms that formerly comprised a chambered series of functional parts of a master suite were re-combined to establish a flowing bedroom area, sizable walk-in closet, master bathroom, and home office—again with an eye toward reinforcing the expression of the post-and-beam construction by replacing horizontal strip windows with floor-to-ceiling glazing.

The homeowners have made a concerted effort to acquire period Mid-Century Modern furnishings to complete the restoration and recreation of their home. The effect has a somewhat déjà vu quality for an architectural style that has once again become classic.

Photography by Russell Abraham

1   Entry porch
2   Main entry
3   Powder room
4   Family entry/mudroom
5   Informal dining
6   Living
7   Kitchen
8   Formal dining
9   Games
10 Family room
11 Closet
12 Master bedroom
13 Master bathroom
14 Nursery (future office)
15 Storage
16 Garage

Floor plan

The Philosophical Carpenter
Reworking Western Themes
Fernau + Hartman

Richard Fernau and Laura Hartman run their small practice out of a compact studio in the Bayside industrial section of Berkeley, California. Their firm's size belies their significance in the architectural world. They are more than local heroes. Fernau + Hartman's architectural creations are recognized as distinctive regionalists by the world's architectural media. Drawing on a rich regional architectural heritage from Bernard Maybeck to William Wurster to Charles Moore, the work of Fernau + Hartman is strongly influenced by the Bay Area Shingle Style tradition. Their houses are more compounds of small outbuildings than singular shells and they challenge the traditional concepts of inside and out and do it with

"They challenge the traditional concepts of inside and out and do it with forms that are sometimes outwardly very traditional."

forms that are sometimes outwardly very traditional. Fernau describes their buildings as "bringing the inside out," with furniture on wheels that can be rolled onto patios and decks through large openings. The space between buildings is sometimes as important as the buildings themselves. Fernau says that their houses all have outside rooms and begin with a landscape strategy.

Fernau + Hartman's work is distinctive for its reworking of traditional forms. Shed roofs shoot out at rakish angles and double as sunshades. Exterior walls seamlessly integrate traditional board and batten with smooth integral color stucco surfaces. Barn-like interiors reveal exposed structures with liberal use of wood and stone. All of their work involves energy conservation and sustainable building concepts. Fernau says that a house they design for the harsh Rocky Mountain climate of Montana will necessarily look and function very differently than one in coastal California. In all of the firm's work there is an intimacy and coziness that is often lacking in most Modern architecture. It is almost as if Fernau + Hartman are stealth Modernists, creating Modern houses that have the look and feel of more traditional ones. It is this architectural sleight-of-hand that gives the work of Fernau + Hartman its strong appeal.

Neither Hartman nor Fernau are natives of northern California, although they received most of their architectural training there and have called the San Francisco Bay Area home since graduate school. Laura Hartman was a bright, artistic young woman who grew up in Charleston, West Virginia, where family visits to the historic houses of the East Coast inevitably began with a journey through the chemical plants and coalfields of the region. The combination was formative. She attended Smith College in central Massachusetts where she developed her interest in fine art and architecture. She took studio courses in both and graduated with a degree in art. Encouraged by a few professors at Smith, she migrated west to attend the graduate architectural program at the University of California at Berkeley and it was here that she met Fernau. Working for the well-known regionalist architect, Joseph Esherick, for one year, which she says was a very valuable experience, she then finished school and travelled to Europe and South Asia to work and study. When she returned to California, she reconnected with Fernau, who had by that time been practicing for several years. He hired her as his first employee and, shortly thereafter, they became partners. In the early years of the firm, Hartman divided her time between the practice and teaching at Berkeley. As the firm grew, she devoted all of her energies to the practice, foregoing her academic vocation.

Richard Fernau was born in Chicago. The family moved back and forth from Illinois to Massachusetts, before finally moving to the San Francisco region when Fernau was starting high school. Fernau credits his mother as having the most influence on his creative proclivities. His father died while he was still young and as a widow, Fernau's mother was forced to support her young children with her creative skills. She was a professional artist and illustrator who dabbled in interior and fashion design, for a while having a custom millinery shop. Fernau remembers his mother's workshop filled with wonderful materials and blocky hat forms. He also had an aunt and uncle in Chicago who worked in advertising and graphic design respectively and he recalls their loft studio, with its arty, edgy collections and creations, as a perfect expression of what we would now call the "Mad Men era." As a high school student in California, he got a job working in residential construction in the upscale town of Woodside and it was here that he was exposed to high-end residential design from a very hands-on perspective.

Fernau attended the University of California at Santa Cruz where he earned a degree in philosophy. He was set to go on to do graduate work in philosophy when his art history professor dissuaded him. The professor told him that he was not an academic in his soul, but a "philosophical carpenter." It did not take a great leap of logic for Fernau to translate the moniker, "philosophical carpenter" into architect. He shifted gears and applied to the University of California's graduate architecture program at Berkeley. He was accepted, earned his professional degree from the College of Environmental Design, and has been a professor there since the 1980s.

Fernau credits much of his firm's early success to luck and timing. At Berkeley, he had done some innovative design work in energy conservation. Jimmy Carter was President and the conservation group,

Friends of the Earth, approached him to come up with a passive solar retrofit for the White House. The proposal received international media attention and put Fernau on the map. Around the same time, he did a restaurant design for a hotdog shop in San Francisco that used a *trompe l'oeil* mural to expand the space. This was a revival of a late-Renaissance technique that was used to create the illusion of space that had not been used commonly in several hundred years. Fernau described the work as a "Post-Modern hotdog." This simple, yet compelling project also received lots of attention and brought the firm some significant commercial work.

Both Fernau and Hartman say they were fortunate to have their studio in a historic residential district where they were surrounded by original works by Bernard Maybeck, Julia Morgan, and Joseph Esherick. They say it was something of a living laboratory of architecture; a place where they could take new clients on walking tours using these historic buildings almost as a portfolio. It was learning design by looking at the masters that later informed and shaped their morphology.

Today, Fernau + Hartman is still a small practice in Berkeley with a satellite office in Montana, but their work comes from around the country and is an interesting mix of institutional and residential. While their institutional and educational work has increased over time, their core interest is designing houses and sustainability is at the core of each of their designs. Creating viable outdoor living spaces for all of their buildings is a key design criterion, whether it is a courtyard for a house in California or a covered porch for a ranch house in Montana. The end results are houses that are broken apart then put back together in ways that stretch the definition of indoor and outdoor space and reinterpret a craftsman aesthetic that Maybeck never could have imagined. While eschewing a style, their look is distinctive and often challenging. The "philosophical carpenter" is constantly pressing the creative envelope with a mix of traditional forms and modernist ideas.

Santa Inez House

The homeowners for this house just east of Santa Barbara are serious art collectors and former gallery owners. The wife is a fine artist who grew up on a farm in England. They wanted to build a small studio and an energy-efficient house in the country that would also function informally as their "gallery." Aware that building on their steep site would inevitably cause serious disruption to the land, the owners asked Fernau + Hartman to have the new house reveal the qualities of the site and create outdoor spaces for both use and contemplation. Strong breezes from the nearby Pacific Ocean can create surprisingly cool afternoons and evenings year round. The exposed and hilly site can be seen from a number of vantage points, which raised concerns from the various governmental regulatory groups.

Notched into a steep hillside, the house was designed as a device to connect to the landscape. By using carefully planned openings to frame views, Fernau + Hartman blurred the distinction between indoor and outdoor rooms. The main volume of the house is an east–west oriented wedge that functions as the dining, living, and gallery space. The kitchen and master bedroom cut into this wedge and extend out to form protected courtyards on the north and south. The studio stands free of the main structure and defines and shelters the entry. Fernau + Hartman designed steel grating to shade outdoor rooms, and operable wood screens provide shelter from western wind. Exterior shading combined with the thin building sections and generous openings keep the house cool despite extreme summer temperatures. Combined with site walls and trellis structures, the landscaping—composed of drought tolerant natives—further defines the outdoor rooms and makes a gradual transition into the natural landscape. The house's distinctive colors were a collaborative effort between Fernau + Harman and client and were all derived from the site geology and natural vegetation. The colors, fragmented massing, and the weaving together of new and existing vegetation create the illusion of the house disappearing into the distance.

Photography by Richard Barnes and Marion Brenner

1   Entry
2   Dining
3   Living
4   Kitchen
5   Bedroom
6   Bathoom
7   Master bedroom
8   Master bathroom
9   Closet
10 Deck
11 Pool

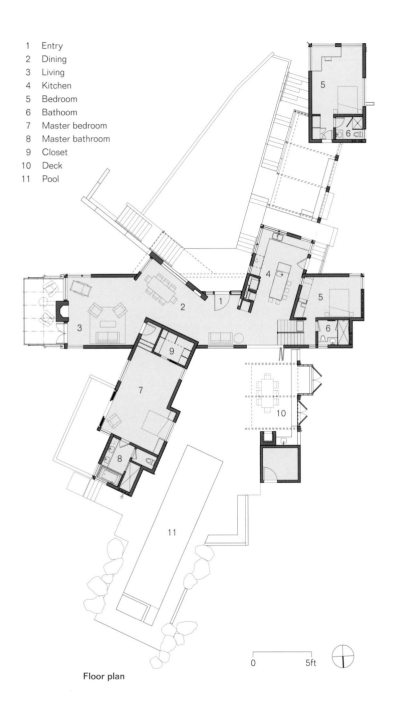

Floor plan

0   5ft

Cookhouse

The Cookhouse represents the culmination of a 15-year design cycle for Fernau + Hartman that began with the renovation of an abandoned homestead in rural Montana, and was followed by the addition and reuse of a number of structures to re-establish a working ranch. Architecturally, the owners wanted a house rooted in the vernacular of rural Montana, not "Western" clichés that gave a movie set appearance. The Cookhouse is now the main residence and the focus of ranch activity; its kitchen and living areas are sized to accommodate extended family dinners and community gatherings.

Renovated over a decade and a half, the compound already contained the 100-year-old ranch house, a granary repurposed as a gym and bunkhouse, and a new car barn. To establish a degree of architectural autonomy, Fernau + Hartman sited the Cookhouse just outside the compound, across a small creek, and connected it to the new equipment barn by a pedestrian bridge. The "creek," which had become little more than a drainage ditch over the years, needed to be restored and was replanted with willows, dogwood, and other native riparian vegetation.

To reduce the scale of the Cookhouse so that it wouldn't dominate the compound, Fernau + Hartman adopted a low one-and-a-half-story gable-roofed structure. Second-story dormers push out from the steep roof to grab light and provide views and summer ventilation. The elongated east–west axis is not only optimal for solar gain, but it also presents the narrow face of the building to the wind and is ideal for mountain views. There is a central circulation spine on both the first and second floor. Generously proportioned, the central hall functions as a gallery for the family's collection of Western art and is arguably the most important gathering space. The circulation spine also functions as a massive duct that connects the entire house to a thermal chimney, which exits the roof at its ridge and keeps the house cool even in the extreme heat of summer, making air-conditioning unnecessary. The house is heated by a ground-source heat pump and energy-efficient wood stoves. Fernau + Hartman gave the roof a substantial overhang that provides cover for a wrap-around porch—an outdoor living space for working and relaxing, protected from the wind, rain, snow, and sun.

Photography by Richard Barnes

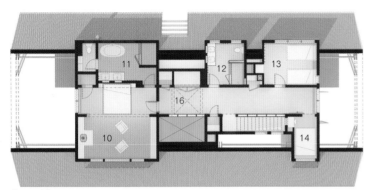

Second floor

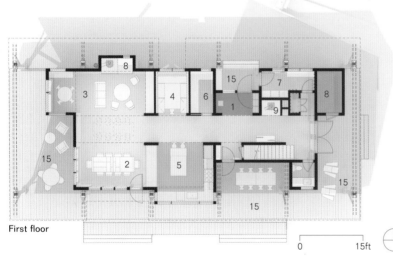

First floor

0   15ft

1	Entry	7	Mudroom	12	Bathroom
2	Dining	8	Utility room	13	Children's bedroom
3	Living	9	Wood-burning stoves	14	Sleeping nook
4	Dining nook	10	Master bedroom with	15	Porch
5	Kitchen		wood-burning stove	16	Cooling chimney
6	Pantry	11	Master bathroom		

Southern Gentleman, Southern Pioneer
Frank Harmon, F.A.I.A.

When I first talked to Frank Harmon about including him in this book, he was both pleased and gracious. He wanted to talk mostly about my work and not his. In his home state of North Carolina, he is something of a legend—the prodigal son who left at an early age to go to the "big city," do well, travel abroad, and then return to practice and teach a new generation of architects. His work is remarkably creative and eclectic, liberally mixing southern architectural tropes with

"It is powerful, modern, and regional all at the same time."

Modern design concepts. His office has done a number of educational and institutional projects, but he has a soft spot for residential work. Scattered around the southeast and the Caribbean, his houses won him the accolade of "Firm of the Year" from *Residential Architect* magazine in 2005. He has become a seminal figure in the architectural world of the southeast, but he would be the last to admit that.

Harmon says he got the architecture bug while staring out the window in his eighth grade classroom at a beautiful house across the street. He was struck by its beauty and simplicity. He wanted to learn how to create that. He started his architectural education at North Carolina State University, but after two years he moved to London to attend the Architectural Association School of Architecture. It was here he was exposed to the great aspiring British architects of the day.

He returned from London to work for Richard Meier in New York, which he did for three years before returning to London to start a practice with some of his old British classmates. His timing was poor. The economy was in bad shape and getting anything built was next to impossible. He supported himself by teaching at the Architectural Association. After 20 years of being away from home, he returned to the United States to assume a teaching role at North Carolina State University, heading their design school. He attributes his respect for regional design to Harwell Hamilton Harris, a well-known California

architect who was one of the leading Modernists in Los Angeles in the 1940s and 1950s. Harris migrated to NC State in the 1960s to teach in their architecture school. He and Harmon became close friends until Harris' death. Harmon likes to quote Harris as saying "the essence of Regionalism was not in its style, but in the resources of the people, their ideas, and their belief in the future." Harmon says he looks westward to California for historical inspiration. He draws a line from Bernard Maybeck and Irving Gill to Rudolph Schindler and Charles Eames to present-day contemporaries like Frank Gehry and Eric Owen Moss, all Californians. While he says the East Coast is too euro-centric to create truly innovative architecture, it is on the East Coast that he lives and works.

It is obvious that Harmon has spent a significant part of his life in the classroom. His manner is that of a venerable academic and his diction is flawless. But unlike other architects who become swaddled in academia, Harmon has continued to practice and to create significant architecture. His works—a mix of commercial, institutional, and residential—win award after award. It is powerful, modern, and regional all at the same time. When asked to talk about regional design, Harmon assured me that he had no interest in the vernacular as a historic style to be copied, but that he was keenly interested in the wisdom and first principles that indigenous architecture has to offer. He then waxed nostalgic about the past, talking about historical buildings in North Carolina that paid keen attention to site weather and environment. He noted that 100 years ago, builders did not have the luxury of HVAC, hermetically sealed buildings, and advanced climate control, so they were forced to pay attention to the environment for their own survival. He argues that architectural reality is being discovered once again in sustainable design. After reading some of the writings of Frank Lloyd Wright two generations removed, I get the impression that I am in the room with one of his disciples.

Ferris Strickland House

The client on this southern butterfly house was an urban couple who were looking for a rural retreat in North Carolina. Their lot bordered a county road and had a steep slope with breathtaking forest views. Harmon's solution was to create a butterfly house that opened up to the forest views and presented a more private face to the road. The client requested a simple structure, one that had little ornamentation and exposed structural elements. Harmon raised the house on large wooden trusses and floated it over the escarpment without cutting a single tree. He gave the north and east faces large floor-to-ceiling windows that captured the forest view.

Harmon's design is a progression from the entrance at the top of the hill, across a bridge and into a balcony foyer, at which point the drama of the scenery outside fills the interior through north-facing glass walls. From the balcony, Harmon created a graceful stair that descends past the glass (in essence, through the trees) to the main living floor, which opens onto a sunny and partially secluded south-facing terrace below the bridge.

At all times of the day, the house is filled with a view of nature and, by day, dappled light. Deep roof overhangs extend a visual link to the outside and shade the glass. Laminated wood columns and beams, plainly bracketed, strengthen the presence of nature, add an element of warmth to the interior, and echo the trees beyond. Careful arrangement of glazing, even on the more private, street-facing elevation, maintains a sense of transparency and lightness. This is consistent throughout the interior: partition walls between rooms stop short of reaching the exposed-wood ceiling and pocket doors between spaces feature "frosted" central panels in the spirit of shoji screens.

The strength of the wood structure contrasts with the delicacy of the environment, framing the expanse of nature and contrasting it with the intimacy of the house. The structure of the house is parallel strand lumber, conserving forest resources. All framing and trim is locally harvested southern yellow pine. Openings are designed to capture prevailing southwesterly breezes and to embrace cool air from the creek valley on summer evenings. From outside at night, the house appears as a fragile, luminous tent cradled by the forest.

Photography by Jeffrey Jacobs

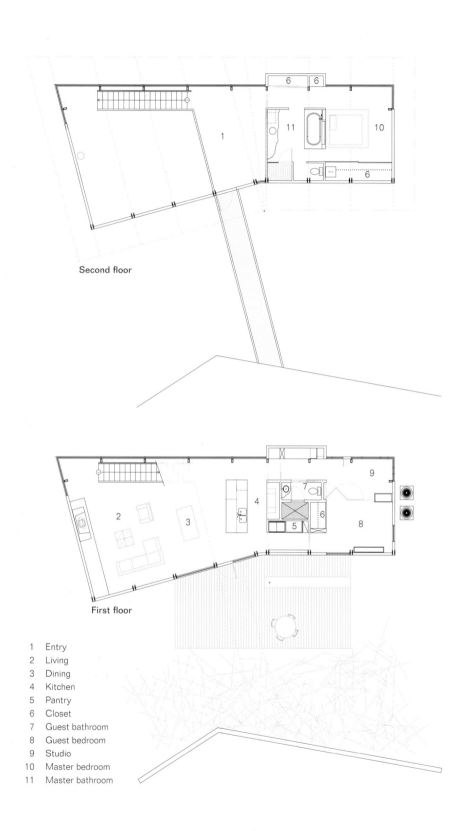

Second floor

First floor

1 Entry
2 Living
3 Dining
4 Kitchen
5 Pantry
6 Closet
7 Guest bathroom
8 Guest bedroom
9 Studio
10 Master bedroom
11 Master bathroom

A Well-Fastened Man

Greg Faulkner Architect

Everything about Greg Faulkner's architecture is well fastened, from the Cor-ten steel exteriors to the stainless and glass balustrades that line the interior passageways. If Mies van der Rohe said "God is in the details," then Greg Faulkner must be a saint. Each surface has its own unique treatment and makes its own statement, from rough textured concrete forms to smooth naturally pigmented plaster walls to room dividers of dark walnut and steel plate. But Faulkner's work is more than a collection of just great details; it is about conventional architectural programs treated in an unconventional way. There is always something unexpected and exciting happening when one walks through one of his houses. Changes of volume, ceiling height, and surface treatment add an element of intrigue and drama to his work that is unique and wonderful. His houses reflect a thoughtfulness that is uncommon in most residential design.

"Changes of volume, ceiling height, and surface treatment add an element of intrigue and drama to his work that is unique and wonderful."

Faulkner grew up in the hardscrabble steel town of Gary, Indiana. His father was an engineer who did design work for a metal fastener company. His grandfather worked in one of the cities great steel mills. As a youth, his grandfather would take him on tours of the mill to watch red-hot steel pouring out of the blast furnace. His father did the same at his bolt-manufacturing plant. Making steel and creating objects out of steel run deep in Faulkner's consciousness.

Being a facile artist, he attended Purdue University and received a degree in industrial illustration. Out of school, he landed a job with a major aircraft manufacturer in Nevada as part of a design team developing a new, carbon fiber body private jet. His work there was a combination of avionics design and industrial drawing. Faulkner's father-in-law ran a large architectural practice in Las Vegas that did educational and institutional work. A tour of his office was all it took for Faulkner's epiphany into architecture. He enrolled in the architecture program at the University

of New Mexico and quickly finished his bachelor's degree in architecture, at which point he returned to Las Vegas to work in his father-in-law's office. It was here that he learned the "nuts and bolts" of building.

Shifting gears and looking for inspiration, he enrolled in the graduate architecture program at Massachusetts Institute of Technology. It was at MIT that he was mentored by Maurice K. Smith, an influential New Zealand architect and educator who espoused a concept of organic architecture. Faulkner says that the prevailing design philosophy was based on an intrinsic respect for the nature of materials and the land or context that the building was to be built in. He says, "We learned an honesty of form and material that was built organically in place as Wright would do." Faulkner describes his MIT experience as life-changing and "amazing."

After MIT, Faulkner worked for a handful of well-established New England firms including Kyu Sung Woo and Ben Thompson before returning to Lake Tahoe. Faulkner describes his migration west as one of following the work. In the midst of an economic downturn, people were still building large ski homes in the Sierra Mountains and he was able to find work there. He opened his own office in the town of Truckee and soon had a steady stream of clients knocking on his door. Faulkner, who has run a successful practice in the Sierra Nevada Mountains for over 20 years, has recently opened a second office in the San Francisco Bay Area. He says that there is a certain freedom in designing houses for coastal California, contrasting the mild, snow-free climate of the Bay Area to the six months of snow fall in the high Sierras. Faulkner's practice is still mostly residential with a mix of hospitality and resort work.

Faulkner has spent much of his professional life living and building in particularly harsh environments; a place where snow loads, heat gain and loss, and seismic activity are serious concerns. Yet his buildings are neither bunkers nor Tyrolean fantasies. They are Modernist takes on traditional mountain home craftsman building types that exude both warmth and wonderment. Incorporating the latest energy-saving technologies and often using sustainable or recycled materials, his houses are a testament to livability.

Butterfly House

This Butterfly-style house is located in a quiet San Francisco suburb surrounded by 1960s-style ranch houses. The owners, a professional couple, owned the existing house and wanted to completely transform it into a highly energy efficient, sustainable building. Their plan was to "deconstruct" the existing home, recycle all of its parts and then build anew. They did exactly that. Ninety percent of the building was either sold off as recycled material or reused and very little of it ended up in the city dump.

By inverting the classic gable roof found on many of the neighborhood's surrounding homes, Faulkner was able to provide visual privacy with high solid walls, and bring in light with clerestory windows that face the busy street. Heat gain is controlled by solar-rated glass and deep eaves that blocked the summer sun. The house opens to a bright courtyard where window walls bring in morning sun to the primary living areas of the kitchen and family room. A courtyard patio is shielded from harsh midday sun by the oversized eaves and provides a comfortable outdoor living space both day and night.

Using both passive heat control design and mechanical energy saving systems, the house is a near net-zero energy user. Rainwater is collected from roof runoff and stored in large cisterns to be later used for washing clothes, secondary sinks, outdoor entry pool, and ultimately landscaping. The house has an operable solar chimney that ventilates the house in the summer.

Photography by Russell Abraham

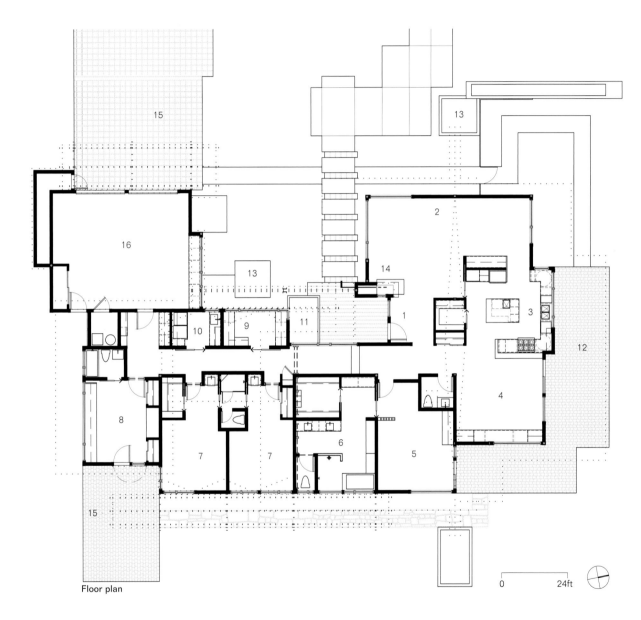

1   Entry
2   Living/dining
3   Kitchen
4   Family room
5   Master bedroom
6   Master bathroom
7   Bedroom
8   Study/guest bedroom
9   Office
10   Laundry
11   Water feature
12   Covered terrace
13   Rainwater collection
14   Solar chimney
15   Sun screen
16   Garage

Floor plan

0   24ft

Livable Modern for the Pacific Northwest
Hutchison & Maul Architecture

Robert Hutchison and Thomas Maul are partners in their eponymously named firm in Seattle, Washington. They have a 12-year-old practice that has designed everything from 100-square-foot (9-square-meter)

"Their buildings ... are simple, elegant works of architecture that can easily stand alone without any explanation, either verbal or aesthetic."

additions to 200,000-square-foot (18,580-square-meter) factories in China, but the majority of their work is regionally based residential architecture. While avowed Modernists, they take an open, non-formulaic approach to each of their projects. No two projects look alike, but each has a strong sense of place and one or two dominant themes or ideas that circumscribe the design and set its parameters. Whether it is an urban infill house or a mountain cabin on 40 acres (16 hectares), each project is infused with a creative spark, a generous imagination, and a regional sensitivity that gives their work character and individuality. Maul likes to refer to their work as livable Modern. Perhaps he is being too modest. Yes, their buildings are both Modern and livable, but they are simple, elegant works of architecture that can easily stand alone without any explanation, either verbal or aesthetic.

Both Hutchison and Maul started life in the eastern part of the United States—Hutchison in Philadelphia and Maul in southern New Jersey. They both studied engineering as undergraduates—Hutchison at Drexel University in Philadelphia and Maul at Bucknell University in central Pennsylvania, where they earned degrees in civil (Maul) and structural and architectural engineering (Hutchison). Hutchison worked as a structural engineer for four years before hearing the clarion call of architecture. After taking several evening courses in architecture at Drexel, he decided to pull up roots and move to the West Coast to earn his professional degree in architecture at the

University of Washington in Seattle. Maul had a more circumlocutious root to the West Coast. His intense interest in food landed him in Vancouver, British Columbia, where he ran a catering company. After spending a few years there, he was offered a job with a startup coffee company as an architect on their fledgling design team. The name of the company was Starbucks. Maul decided that he really needed a professional architectural degree and enrolled at the University of Washington in Seattle. It was here that he met Hutchison. Ironically, both men grew up 50 miles apart and only met and became friends and partners 3,000 miles away in graduate school.

Hutchison and Maul continued to work while going to school and after graduating worked for larger Seattle-based architectural firms doing a variety of projects. Hutchison became a project manager at The Miller Hull Partnership while Maul got a position at GGLO working on retail and commercial projects. Together with a group of other University of Washington graduates, they formed an architectural interest group called *rectifier* which undertook hypothetical projects focusing on the adaptive reuse of urban spaces and structures in Seattle. The group gave the participants a chance to "talk about architecture in a meaningful way outside of their respective firms," says Hutchison. *rectifier* generated some local recognition and design awards, but no commissions. Both Hutchison and Maul completed graduate fellowships in Scandinavia and they each agree that living in northern Europe and studying architecture there was a transformational experience. It was also a common experience that strengthened their friendship. In 2001, without any significant clients in hand, both Hutchison and Maul decided it was time to start their own firm. Their beginnings were modest, but since then they have slowly built a strong practice completing over 100 projects.

Today, Hutchison & Maul Architecture has become a significant voice among small and mid-sized architectural firms in the Pacific Northwest. Their projects embody the region's forward-thinking, techno-centric culture and its spectacular, visually stimulating environment of lush forests, snow capped mountains and expansive inland waters. Maul describes the firm "as clearly contemporary, of and with the time. We deal with existing sites, materials, and technology that are available to us today. And we are forming it for the way people live today. Clearly our projects are livable. Our work lends itself to real people living in real spaces. It is not precious; it is not untouchable." Hutchison and Maul, designing simple and practical modern architecture to meet the needs of their real world clients. What's not to like?

Lake House on Lake Washington

The Lake House is a very small, elegant, beach-front guesthouse that fronts onto Lake Washington. The house is only 900 square feet (83 square meters) and consists of three rooms, a covered patio, and a quiet hillside courtyard garden. The client for this project was fascinated with the idea of using copper siding on the house and letting it age naturally. Hutchison and Maul found a source left over from the construction of a new Federal Courthouse in downtown Seattle. Ultimately, that did not work out, but another source was located and the walls, roof, and ceiling of the ground floor covered patio were sheathed in naturally aging copper. The architects created front and rear outdoor living spaces by cutting into a steep hillside and then lifting the house and creating a covered patio that faces the lake. Hutchison and Maul's simple, folded plate design with its russet-hued cladding slips quietly into the very narrow site and creates a rich variety of both outdoor venues and lake views for the owners.

Photography by Alan Abramowitz

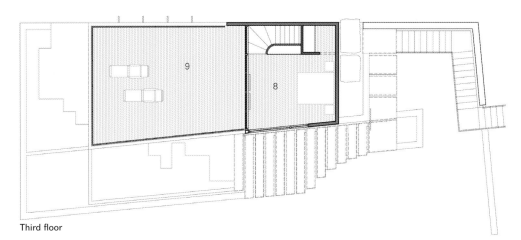

Third floor

Second floor

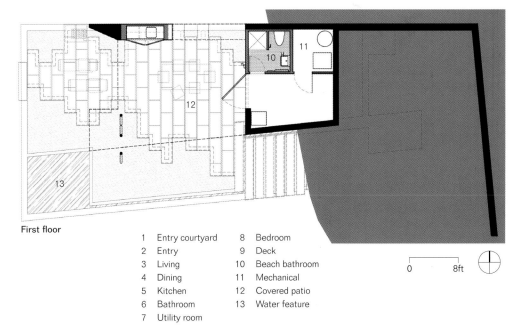

First floor

1	Entry courtyard	8	Bedroom
2	Entry	9	Deck
3	Living	10	Beach bathroom
4	Dining	11	Mechanical
5	Kitchen	12	Covered patio
6	Bathroom	13	Water feature
7	Utility room		

0   8ft

Livable Modern for the Pacific Northwest   99

A Young Firm with Fresh Ideas
Feldman Architecture

Jonathan Feldman might have been an astronomer. He might even have been an English professor. After all, those were his undergraduate majors at Amherst College in Massachusetts. But luckily for the world of architecture, those were only starting points in a young career that has more than its share of successful, award-winning projects. Feldman has begun to create a unique design presence in a very crowded world of small firms doing residential work in northern California. His firm has grown from a one-man office operating out of his basement in San Francisco to a 16-person firm in the toney North Beach neighborhood. Feldman's work is a good fit for his urbane California clients. It is modern, sustainable, individualistic, and quirky. He creates an architecture that challenges the imagination and gives us something warm and familiar at the same time. Whether it is roofs that become gardens or building shapes that squiggle like caterpillars, the firm's work is always refreshing and new.

"His design values are rooted, however, in basic Modernist concepts: having structure express itself, simplifying forms, integrating inside and outside spaces."

Feldman started life in New England and spent his formative years in Palo Alto, California. When time for college arrived, he chose the coziness of a small liberal arts education in New England over the large, factory-like institutions in California. He studied astronomy and English and jokes that astronomy has become very useful for designing buildings. Knowing what the sun's angles are on any particular day can be a key design consideration. After college, he migrated to Los Angeles and did a stint in the film industry working as a production assistant. He soon realized that he could only make it in that business if he lived in Los Angeles—a problem, since he did not like that city. On a backpacking trip in Utah, he met some architects working in a small town. It was an epiphany—here was a career that

one could practice and not be in a major metropolis. He applied to the architecture school at the University of Oregon and was accepted into their master's program. He says that Oregon was a good place to be because there was no overarching design philosophy, just a healthy variety of design cultures. "I left Oregon with no answers, just good questions," he says. Returning to the Bay Area, Feldman began working for a series of smaller firms where he learned the everyday basics of running an office. In 2003 he started his own firm in the basement of a house he remodeled. He got some recognition from this first residential project and his firm grew from there. By 2007, he had enough work to move out of his house and into a conventional office.

Feldman says his approach to architecture is "holistic." He loves working on everything from the overall design to the smallest details. Insisting that he doesn't have a style *per se*, he strives for a consistency in his work. He enjoys working on an older building in an urban setting as much as creating a new building on a pristine rural site. His design values are rooted, however, in basic Modernist concepts: having structure express itself, simplifying forms, integrating inside and outside spaces. Feldman says that working on lower budget projects forced him to think creatively and design economically. "If it looks simple, natural and easy, then that is probably the best design," he says, a big fan of some modern regionalist architects who have labored to tie their work to the site and adapt to the environment.

Just by looking at his work, it is hard to put a label on the architecture of Jonathan Feldman. He is clearly a regional Modernist, but his work goes beyond that simple label. It is infused with a delicacy and individuality that is uncommon in the genre. He is a young architect whose firm has created some memorable buildings. One can only speculate that he has a bright future with his best work yet before him.

Caterpillar House

Caterpillar House is sited in the Santa Lucia Preserve, a spectacular bit of open-space development about 150 miles south of San Francisco. Unlike many of its more conservative neighbors, this house is neither pretentious nor large. In a development of mostly very large Spanish-style homes on huge lots, the Caterpillar House is the exception. Its inspiration was drawn from the Modernist ranch houses of the 1950s and 1960s. It truly is an homage to economical and ecological building. To say that the house is "built into the land" is an understatement. The house's rammed earth walls come from the earth that it sits on. Its roof catches rainwater that is stored in large cisterns and used for landscaping during the long California dry season. The fenestration is designed to passively heat in the winter and cool in the summer. The house has moveable sunshades that extend in the summer months and contract in the winter. The house's sinuous shape contours to the hill's undulations and was Feldman's way of translating the owner's desire for a curved house. Integrated photovoltaic panels enable the house to produce all of its energy requirements without compromising the graceful curve of the low roof against the hill.

The Caterpillar House is proof that ecological design can be both practical and beautiful at the same time.

Photography by Joe Fletcher

1   Entry
2   Gallery
3   Dining
4   Living
5   Kitchen
6   Closet
7   Powder room
8   Master bedroom
9   Master bathroom
10   Office
11   Guest bathroom
12   Guest bedroom
13   Laundry/mudroom
14   Courtyard
15   Water storage tanks
16   Terrace
17   Garage
18   Driveway

0   12ft

Floor plan

Husband and Wife Design Team
Kwan Henmi Associates

Kwan Henmi Associates has grown from a small husband-and-wife architectural team into one of San Francisco's larger design firms. Their practice spreads over a variety of disciplines on both the public and private sides of the ledger. They are both avowed Modernists with a penchant for Mid-Century Modern ideals and designs. Infused in their work is a quirky regional identity that is probably best expressed in some of their residential and multi-family work. Stylistically and thematically, they have done a little of everything from retro-industrial condos on the east side of San Francisco Bay to Modernist high-rises in downtown San Francisco to colorful Latin-themed projects in the region's Hispanic quarters. All exhibit a lively character and respect for culture and place which are hallmarks of the firm's work.

Sylvia Kwan was born in Hong Kong and emigrated to the U.S. when she was eight years old. She comes from a long line of architects in China where her granduncle and his brothers ran what was known as the SOM of China in the early to mid-1900s. She started taking drafting classes in high school—often the only girl in the class—and enrolled in the architecture program at the University of California, Berkeley, earning her bachelor and master's degrees there. It was here that she met her future husband, Denis Henmi, who had transferred into architecture from

> *"All exhibit a lively character and respect for culture and place which are hallmarks of the firm's work."*

a pre-dentistry program. Kwan jokes that dentistry and architecture are similar, just design on a different scale. Kwan was fortunate to find work right out of college, first interning for the well-known firm, Marquis Associates, and later working for Gensler where she did space planning and some large-scale architectural projects. She left Gensler after two years and set up a small office in her apartment working on small jobs that her now-husband, Henmi, was not able to do because of his full-time employment with a large civil engineering firm.

Denis Henmi grew up in a suburb on the east side of San Francisco Bay. His Japanese-American father wanted him to become a dentist, but after two years in the pre-dental program at the University of California, Berkeley he switched to architecture. After earning his professional degree there, he found a role in a large civil engineering firm where he was the only architect, working there for 10 years before finally leaving to start his own firm with Kwan. The land planning work from his civil engineering job grew into larger development work in the burgeoning Silicon Valley region of the San Francisco Bay Area and they designed office buildings for companies including Apple and DEC, soon moving into multi-family housing. Kwan, always the social activist, developed a reputation in public sector architecture. Being something of a gender pioneer and activist, she was able to bring in interesting public work such as schools, senior housing, and transit projects.

A few years ago, a developer client commissioned them to design a large-scale second home residential project in Moab, near the picturesque Arches Canyon area of southern Utah. Kwan says the firm prides itself on being urban-oriented, working mostly on "brown field" sites rather than "green fields." But the Moab project was different. The project entailed a considerable amount of naturalist restoration of the semi-arid area, which had been abused for years by off-road vehicle traffic, in addition to some sophisticated land planning to preserve the site's natural beauty while adding 50 home sites. This was a development project with a major conservationist component. With his background in civil engineering, Henmi was well suited for this project. The firm hired biologists and arborists to develop a restoration plan for the site, planting thousands of native cacti and building foot trails throughout the site.

Moab House

The Moab House was commissioned by the project's developer to be a signature architectural statement that would hopefully set the bar for the entire development. The site was a difficult one, a cliff that dropped 200 feet (60 meters), but afforded spectacular views of the opposing canyons and distant mountains. Henmi's solution was to have the house step down the hillside three stories, with the top story limited to a double garage and hidden from the roadway. Access was gained from crossing a bridge and then dropping one story into the living room on the second floor, where most of the house's public spaces were located. The glass wall in the main living space yielded a view that was almost like a living mural, changing hour by hour as the sun angled around the canyon's salmon-colored walls.

Henmi created hidden courtyards against the canyon walls using the natural stone as a backdrop. On the first floor he built a small lap pool that straddled the width of the house from the canyon wall in the rear to a small deck on the north side. Henmi capped the large glass expanses with a deep metal-covered sun shade that spanned the entire upper floor, and used native stone to veneer the walls and help anchor the house into its desert site.

Kwan Henmi has helped dispel the belief that eco-friendly building has to be basic or unimaginative. Moab House is dramatic and spectacular in its views as well as in its use of indigenous materials.

Photography by Russell Abraham

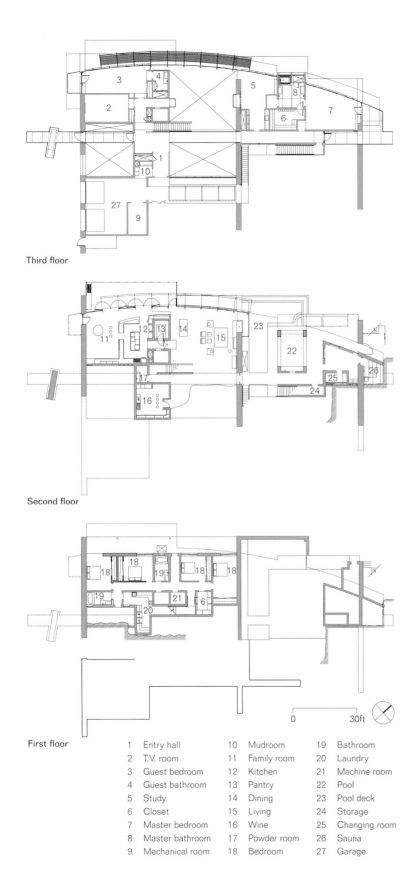

Third floor

Second floor

First floor

1	Entry hall	10	Mudroom	19	Bathroom
2	T.V. room	11	Family room	20	Laundry
3	Guest bedroom	12	Kitchen	21	Machine room
4	Guest bathroom	13	Pantry	22	Pool
5	Study	14	Dining	23	Pool deck
6	Closet	15	Living	24	Storage
7	Master bedroom	16	Wine	25	Changing room
8	Master bathroom	17	Powder room	26	Sauna
9	Mechanical room	18	Bedroom	27	Garage

0   30ft

Looking Backwards and Forwards

Arcanum Architecture

Arcanum Architecture is a partnership comprising three architects from different parts of California who traveled to San Francisco to set up shop. Tim Chappelle, Anthony Fish, and Kurt Simrock all

"They take the quintessential gabled-roof country house and strip it to its bare essentials, then rework its forms to come up with something that is both historic and modern at the same time."

started life in different parts of California and went to either the University of Southern California or California Polytechnic State University at San Luis Obispo. Chappelle says he always wanted to be an architect. His dad was an engineer and architecture was a natural fit. After college, the three partners independently migrated north to work for the large, diverse San Francisco firm Backen Arrigoni & Ross (BAR Architects). It was here that they met each other, polished their design skills, and started their own firm in 1996. Their first clients were from the hospitality and retail trades. Designing restaurants in the food mecca of San Francisco can be a rewarding field. Anthony Fish managed the hospitality side of the business while Tim Chappelle and Kurt Simrock expanded the firm's scope into residential work. As the economy and markets shifted, their work went from 80 percent commercial to 80 percent residential.

Over the years, Arcanum Architecture has developed a distinctive and sought-after look that has a comfortable feel for Northern Californian sensibilities. Chappelle insists that all three partners are dedicated Modernists, yet their work is built of familiar natural materials and their design tropes are more farmhouse than Bauhaus. They take the quintessential gabled-roof country house and strip it to its bare essentials, then rework its forms to come up with something that is both historic and Modern at the same time. As Chappelle says, traditional 19th-century house design was from the outside in. By contrast, most 20th-century design was from the inside out with less sophistication, adding style as ornament to the exteriors. Their work tries to combine both concepts in a rational and balanced way. As with many Californian architects, integrating outside spaces with interiors is a key design theme. Many of their houses have enclosed courtyards or window walls that open onto dramatic vistas. Often, Chappelle will wrap a house in a fairly traditional shell exterior and then revert to a Bauhaus-like minimalist interior, exposing rough structural elements when appropriate. A gabled-roof exterior often gives way to a very contemporary collection of interior spaces with varied ceiling heights and volumes. Sliding barn doors, board and batten exteriors, and multi-paned windows sheath dramatic and loft-like interiors with soaring ceilings and foldaway window walls. These are houses that fit into traditional neighborhoods yet give the homeowners the excitement of living in a contemporary space.

Arcanum Architecture's houses are both modern and traditional by design. They freely take rural 19th-century design tropes and give them a 21st-century remake that is both tasteful and fun.

Felton Gables House

This house was an infill project in an established San Francisco Bay Area suburban neighborhood. The community had strict design guidelines to preserve sunlight access and property coverage, and the owners were an interesting couple with a strong design sense. The wife was a realtor who wanted a house that fit into the neighborhood, while the husband was an industrial designer who was, in no small part, responsible for the products of the world's most famous technology company. Simply put, she wanted a farmhouse and he wanted a white box. Chappelle's solution was to give them both.

With a few quirky details, the house presents itself to the street as a well-tailored cottage while being anything but. Inside, rough-hewn spaces of poured-in-place concrete and stark white plaster walls connect together in a U-shape around an intimate internal courtyard. In order to conform to building height restrictions, one-third of the house is below grade and light wells bring daylight to the lower level. The upper levels are laid out in a traditional format around the central courtyard and are drenched in California's abundant sunshine. The industrial designer husband designed some of the unique bath fixtures in the house and not surprisingly, they looked very much like his white-boxed computers and phones. Situated on a relatively small lot, the house makes judicious use of space and has the feel of a much larger house. The Felton Gables House is Modern architecture working in stealth mode.

Photography by Russell Abraham

Second floor

1 Entry
2 Living
3 Dining
4 Kitchen
5 Family room
6 Mudroom
7 Powder room
8 Utility room
9 Master bedroom
10 Master bathroom
11 Bedroom
12 Bathroom
13 Outdoor court
14 Garage

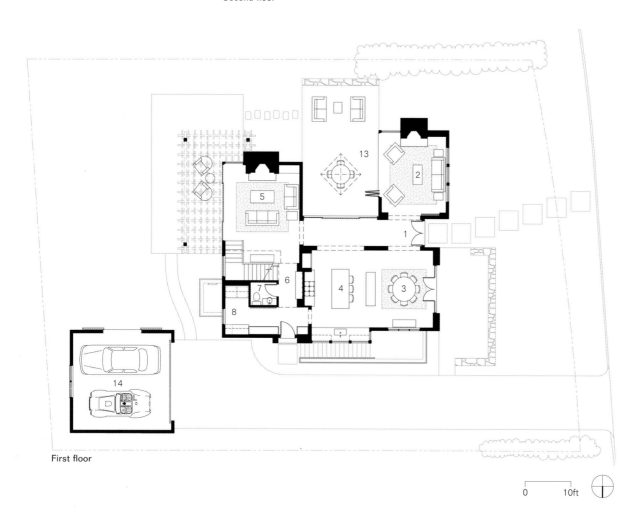

First floor

0   10ft

Texas Originals
Lake | Flato

Texas is large enough to be a country. Its climate and terrain is as varied as its citizens. Its southeastern edge is almost subtropical while its western border is a semi-arid plain. Known for its boisterous, self-assured politicians and spicy hot barbeque, it is easy to characterize all Texas as overstated and unsophisticated.

> *"Characterized as an environmentally friendly design firm, Lake | Flato occupies a rare spot in the architectural world."*

But, like most generalities, this simplistic view of Texas is just that. Texas has a rich history and vibrant multicultural population. It is home to a number of new industries and important centers of learning. In addition to being the United States' largest oil-producing region, it is also home to the largest high-technology industry outside of California. It is here in San Antonio, Texas' second largest city, that Lake | Flato have their office and run a bustling practice that is anything but a Texas stereotype.

Characterized as an environmentally friendly design firm, Lake | Flato occupies a rare spot in the architectural world. Their work is Modern, vernacular, and "green." Their buildings, whether a single family residence or an entire college campus, manage to make strong statements about sustainability, Modernism, and respect for regional design tastes. The uneven gable roofs, the lathe screen, the enclosed courtyard all remind us of a vernacular theme. But Lake | Flato's work is only informed by history, not bound by it. It is as fresh and as Modern as today. There is a lightness and transparency to their work, which runs counter to most thematic Texas stereotypes. Their vision extends beyond individual buildings to land planning concepts that endeavor to make cities more compact and people-friendly places where people can live work and play in close proximity. Interestingly, they still do a significant amount of residential work in Texas and

throughout the southwest. Their residential work is constantly cited for its environmental sensitivity as well as its handsome design. For Lake | Flato, their residential projects are a laboratory of expression and architectural experimentation; a place to develop good ideas for larger works.

Both Ted Flato and David Lake are native Texans. Flato grew up in the Gulf city of Corpus Christi while Lake is a native of Austin. Flato's father was a local real estate developer who was fond of sailing. Flato says he spent many hours sailing on Corpus Christi Bay discussing the shoreline's potential. Flato's family also owned some rural land in Texas' hill country, a place where he spent his summer vacations. It was here that the young Flato gained an appreciation for Texas' natural beauty and a sense of conservation. Lake grew up in Austin where he developed an appreciation for local prairie style vernacular buildings that dotted the surrounding rural landscape. He stayed close to home for his education, earning his architecture degree from the University of Texas at Austin while Flato ventured west to California and Stanford University to earn his. Lake started his career designing and building solar-powered adobe houses in the Texas Panhandle. In 1979, he joined the firm of Ford Powell Carson in San Antonio and Flato joined shortly thereafter. O'Neil Ford has been described as the most famous "unknown architect" of the Mid-Century Modernist era. Largely self-taught, Ford blended an Arts and Crafts style with Texas regionalism and Modernism to create a uniquely Southwestern architectural trope. Flato remembers Ford as a great inspiration and a great counterpoint to what he'd learned at Stanford. He would say things like "that looks great, but how are you going to put a roof on it." It was in Ford's office that Lake and Flato met and began their lifelong partnership. Ford died in 1982 and in 1984 Lake and Flato decided to open their own office. Flato talks about the firm's

early years with a sense of both pride and wonderment. He says, "We were young, but we had a number of small residential projects. These projects celebrated the outdoors. They were houses, but they were houses where people were making a choice to go to the outdoors. They were very sustainable. The design was how you can live as closely to the outdoors as possible and create a building that responds to the climate."

Sustainability and environmental awareness have always been a part of Lake | Flato's work. From Lake's early sod house experiments to a new campus for the University of Arizona, blending buildings with the natural environment has been a driving force. Flato says that they like to use passive design elements, like sunshades and screens to control the environment. Lake takes an even broader view. He says, "The built environment has such an enormous impact on the natural environment. I started my career dedicated to designing buildings that were intrinsically a part of their place; buildings that were climatically attuned, energy-efficient and resource-efficient."

Interestingly, while environmental awareness and sustainability have gone in and out of fashion over the past 30 years, Lake | Flato have been singular in their work. Their blend of southwest vernacular with energy-stingy building designs and a healthy dose of 21st-century Modernism is exceptional. It is Modern architecture with a regional flavor and a strong grounding in sensible passive energy design. O'Neil Ford would be proud.

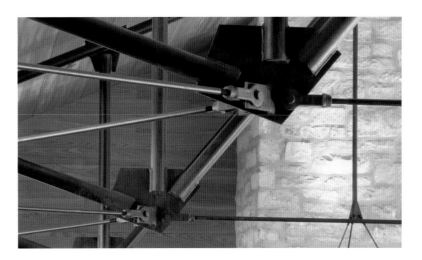

Cross Timbers Ranch House

Located in northern Texas, Cross Timbers is a ranch house that was developed by the owners as both a vacation home and company retreat. The ranch is a working cattle ranch that had been in the family for a generation. Ted Flato worked with his associates, Bill Aylor and Ryan Jones, to design the house as a compound with four independent structures navigating a tree-lined ridge and separating pasture and an adjacent valley. The owners wanted the house to fit into the pastoral setting but still make a strong architectural statement. Flato's team came up with a plan that gave each structure a specific purpose: a primary residence, guesthouse, game room/pavilion, and wine cellar/overlook. Breaking the design into several structures allowed the project to frame outdoor rooms, collect breezes, and integrate itself with the surrounding landscape. It also enabled the owner to control energy usage by limiting the use of lighting and mechanical systems for programmed areas during the majority of the year. The house uses 100 percent closed pond-loop geothermal technology for its HVAC systems. Natural breezes are highlighted by the porches, dogtrot decks, and walkways that connect the structures to one another as well as to the surrounding landscape. The structures are finished similarly to the modest structures that are found on the surrounding ranch—steel pipe fencing, wood clad barns, and corrugated metal shade structures.

The owners, Laura and Greg Bird, are quite fond of their rustic modern retreat. As Laura says, "I love the fact that when you get here, you immediately relax. It has something to do with the way the architecture blends with the landscape." Taking vernacular forms and reworking them with a Modern twist is what Lake | Flato do with a passion.

Photography by Frank Ooms

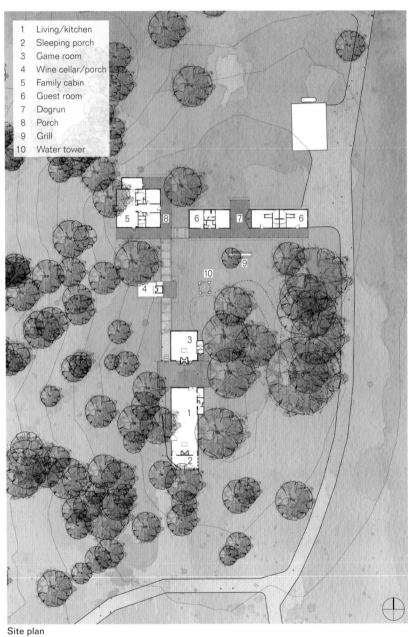

1 Living/kitchen
2 Sleeping porch
3 Game room
4 Wine cellar/porch
5 Family cabin
6 Guest room
7 Dogrun
8 Porch
9 Grill
10 Water tower

Site plan

Two Faces of the Same Firm
Min | Day

Min | Day is a small architectural firm that lives in two worlds: coastal California and the Midwestern heartland of Nebraska. The two partners, E.B. Min and Jeffrey Day, each run separate offices in two distinctly different parts of the country. The scope of their work is

"Min | Day's work is not 'thinking outside the box.' It is disassembling 'the box' and then putting it back together in a whole new way."

almost as varied as their locations. From high tech offices for Silicon Valley startups in California to institutional work for non-profit art foundations in Nebraska, to highly experimental and conceptual work in both locales. It is hard to put a label on their work. It is very avant-garde without calling excessive attention to itself. There is an organic, non-linear quality to their designs that speaks more to Frank Lloyd Wright than Mies van der Rohe. Non-rectilinear spaces are divided with sinuous screens cut from plywood or fiberboard made of recycled materials. Exposed concrete shells are met with smooth, colorful plasterboard surfaces. One can easily say that Min | Day's work is not "thinking outside the box." It is disassembling "the box" and then putting it back together in a whole new way.

E.B. Min grew up in the south and western United States. An art enthusiast from a young age, she went to Brown University to study art and found herself taking architectural studios across the street at Rhode Island School of Design. After graduating she migrated west with a college friend to find work and eventually enrolled in the graduate architecture program at the University of California at Berkeley.

Jeffrey Day grew up in Maine. Min relates that he knew he wanted to be an architect since he was twelve. He received his bachelor's degree in visual studies from Harvard and went on to get his

professional architectural degree from the University of California at Berkeley. It was at Berkeley that Min and Day met. Min says, "Berkeley taught you how to think. When you got to work, you learned how to do it."

Min held a variety of short-term positions before she landed a job with Delaney and Cochran, a well-regarded landscape architecture firm in San Francisco. It was here that she learned the basics of how to build things, how to work with clients, and how to take risks in design. In 1998, Min decided to leave Delaney and Cochran and start her own firm. Day was living in Nebraska at the time and was also ready to start a partnership. Even though they were separated by over 2,000 miles, they decided to create the firm with two offices in 2003. Min says that even though they are different people, their approach to design is on the same path, with the firm both practical and inventive, and willing to try new things.

In some ways, Min | Day might be the prototypical firm of the future—a small footprint operation that can function across continents using all of the tremendous telecommunication methods available today. In the course of one day they can be working on a project in Chicago, a tenant improvement job in San Francisco, and a competition in China, electronically bouncing work from office to office. The most remarkable thing about the firm is how different each project looks. It is a testament to their collective creativity that there is no obvious design signature to their work. Sustainability and energy conservation are always integrated into each project, but these design constraints do not control the look of the final project. Their work exudes a creative, imaginative energy that makes them stand out from the crowd as one of the outstanding young firms in the United States.

Lake Okoboji House

This house is located on a lake in the upper Midwest, an area noted for its glacial lake formations created by the last Ice Age many thousands of years ago. The lake is one of a series of lakes surrounded by farmland that are used primarily as recreation areas for nearby city dwellers. The clients were a professional couple who wanted a lakeside retreat that looked and functioned like none of the other prototypical suburban houses adjacent to the water. They held a small competition among hand-selected firms to come up with a schematic plan for their house. Min and Day spent several weekends at the site evaluating its potential. The plan they came up with was designed to maximize lake views and access while preserving the numerous native burr oaks on the site.

This house was designed as an oversized vacation home that could accommodate large groups of relatives and friends who might come by for extended summer stays. Using a somewhat conventional program,

they placed the major public spaces on the ground floor and gave them lake views with fold-back window walls and a handsome deck. The private sleeping quarters were placed on the upper floor with a great room above the garage that could serve as either a game room or sleeping quarters for young guests. The master bedroom has casework and custom furniture designed by Min | Day. Using a CNC router, they created a giant three-dimensional water drop pattern for the master bed headboard, the rear side of which became cabinets. Minimalist interiors of polished concrete floors and plasterboard walls stand in strong contrast to the majestic oaks and lake just outside the windows.

In an area known more for its uniformity than innovation, the Lake Okoboji house makes an exceptional individualistic statement.

Photography by David Crosby

Second floor

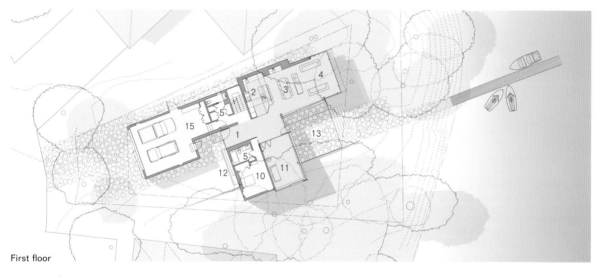

First floor

1 Entry
2 Kitchen
3 Dining
4 Living
5 Bathroom
6 Bunk room
7 Utility
8 Play
9 Study
10 Bedroom
11 Screened porch
12 Skylight
13 Terrace
14 Wood terrace
15 Garage

Basement

0   25ft

138 Rural Modern

A New Face for the Northwest
mw | works architecture and design

mw | works architecture and design is a partnership of two young Seattle architects, Eric Walter and Steve Mongillo. The practice was founded in 2007 and has just started to get recognition for its work. Their houses are a Pacific Northwest regional version of Modern design, a blend of Bauhaus Modern with a lust for natural materials and a clear love of craft. Their portfolio of built work is growing and

"If there was a word for a style that was about clean spaces and natural daylight strategies, that would be what we do."

completed projects thus far exhibit a classy and fresh approach to Modern architecture. They say that they have just started attracting clients who understand what they do and appreciate their organic approach to Modern design. Working in a region of the U.S. with a strong local design tradition, mw | works has found a way to separate itself from the competition.

Both Walter and Mongillo have lived in the region for some time. Walter is a native of Washington, having grown up in a rural community about an hour north of Seattle and Mongillo grew up near San Francisco but migrated to the Northwest to study architecture. Walter's father was a forester who had a woodshop, a place where he spent many hours making things. His father's family was from northern Idaho and as a child he made the trip across the state regularly to a small cabin built by his grandparents. The eastern side of the Cascades is high prairie—stark grasslands punctuated by a solitary barn or farm structure, and those solitary vernacular buildings left a lasting impression.

Mongillo's father was a Silicon Valley engineer. Although he grew up in a somewhat monolithic suburb, many of his friends lived in Eichler houses in Palo Alto. An Eichler house was something of a California phenomenon: Mid-Century Modern merchant-built houses designed by some of the leading Modernist architects of the day and then mass-produced. Eichler lifted a page from the Case Study Houses style-book and then figured out a way to replicate them for the masses. The concepts of indoor–outdoor living, walls of glass, and open flowing spaces exemplified in the Eichler houses were not lost on Mongillo. In high school, he took a course in architectural design and his interest shifted from engineering to architecture, leading him to enroll in the architecture school at the University of Oregon. Upon graduating, he migrated to Massachusetts to work for a non-profit organization focused on ecological architecture. After a year, he returned to the Northwest to accept a position with Cutler Anderson and later Bohlin Cywinski Jackson in their newly established Seattle office.

Walter channeled his childhood interest in building things into a degree in architecture at the University of Washington in Seattle. He went on to earn his master's degree at MIT, a transformational experience. He returned to Seattle to work for a variety of architectural firms before joining Bohlin Cywinski Jackson. It was here he met Mongillo, where they were both working on residential and institutional projects. After five years at Bohlin Cywinski Jackson, they decided to leave and form their own firm, calling themselves mw | works. The recession of 2008 hit just after they founded the firm and it taught them to be flexible, helping them focus their efforts on strong relationships with clients and good design.

Today their firm is thriving in a regional market that appreciates good design and all things modern. While still mostly residential, they have ventured out into rehab and commercial work. Mongillo says, "I think we have a link to Northwest architecture. I think Northwest houses have a lot more to do with materials and craft than other regions. What we are really interested in is the nature of the space and how the light works and how the building fits into the landscape. If there was a word for a style that was about clean spaces and natural daylight strategies, that would be what we do." Walter chimes in, "We are taking influences from this region and applying them to Modernism." It sounds like they are defining the eponymous title of this book without giving it a name.

Case Inlet House

The house sits on a 20-acre (8-hectare) site on the Key Peninsula overlooking the Case Inlet on Puget Sound and beyond the Olympic Mountains to the west. The owners had been coming to the site for several years, visiting in summers to camp in the sunny meadow along the ridge and paddle the Sound from the end of the winding path below.

When they were ready to build a permanent cabin, the relationship between the house and the land was very clear. mw|works was asked to create a modern but simple retreat that would at once provide a sense of shelter and refuge but also be very transparent, taking advantage of both the western views and the southern connections to the meadow. They designed the house to be comfortable for just two but also flexible and at ease entertaining larger groups of family and friends as needed.

mw|works' solution was a house of simple forms that unfolds into the landscape, offering a unique interaction with the natural beauty of the site. A broad flat roof slides high over the living space, unifying the various forms and providing shelter for the exterior deck and barbecue. The living and dining space projects west into the tree canopy on a cantilevered platform, capturing views of the water and the sunset. The kitchen shares those views but the ipe decking (a sustainable Brazilian hardwood) of its floor extends south beyond a sliding glass wall to engage the meadow and the afternoon sun. In the master suite, a notch is removed from the building to create an outdoor room. With a skylight overhead and a glazed floor-to-ceiling pocket door toward the view, this room has become the owners' favorite spot to enjoy a glass of wine at day's end.

With a balance of simple lines and rugged, low maintenance materials, mw|works has created a modest and inviting retreat that is a welcome sanctuary from the city.

Photography by Jeremy Bitterman

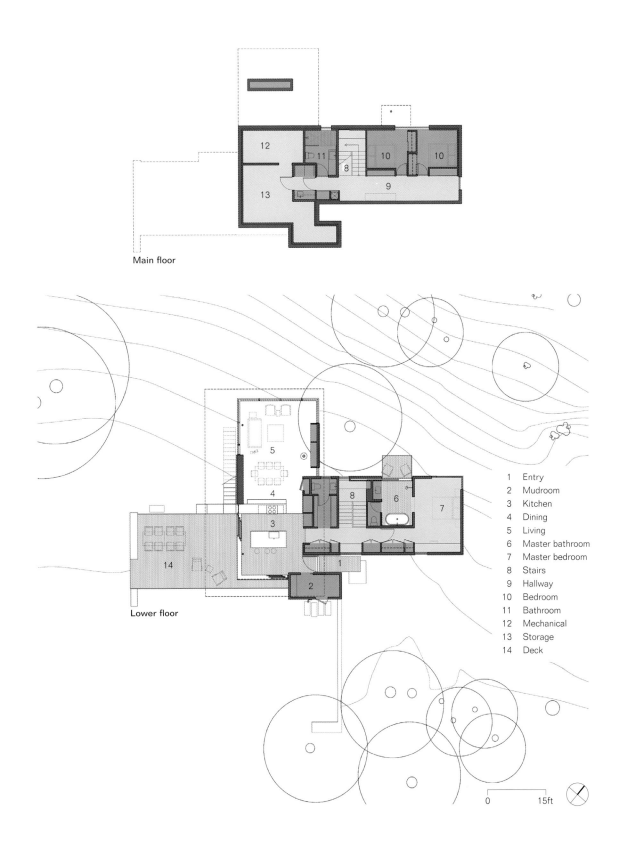

Main floor

Lower floor

1 Entry
2 Mudroom
3 Kitchen
4 Dining
5 Living
6 Master bathroom
7 Master bedroom
8 Stairs
9 Hallway
10 Bedroom
11 Bathroom
12 Mechanical
13 Storage
14 Deck

0   15ft

Northwest Pioneers
Olson Kundig

Jim Olson and Tom Kundig have been partners for over 20 years. They have established themselves as one of the leading architectural firms in North America. Their look is a careful blend of Modernist concepts with Pacific Northwest vernacular architecture. The end result is an architecture that is inviting, sensitive, respectful of its place, and

"Olson's artistic sensibilities paired with Kundig's mechanical genius have resulted in a distinctive regional architecture that both celebrates the physical beauty of the Northwest and lives compatibly with its environment."

clearly Modern. Today, the firm has grown to 100 employees and has a rich mix of commercial, institutional, and residential work. In spite of this, the firm has not forgotten its humble "cabin design" roots that Olson established in 1960s when he built the first cabin on his family's land of Puget Sound just west of Seattle. He has been adding to and changing that original cabin for the last 50 years.

The Pacific Northwest of the United States is one of the wetter places in North America. With latitudes well above 45°N, the region is known for long summer days and wet, cold, and dark winters—not an inviting environment for Bauhaus-inspired glass boxes with flat roofs. Given these environmental extremes, Olson Kundig has found a way to take Modernist concepts and adopt them to the climate and spectacular terrain of the region. In Olson Kundig's houses, flat roofs have given way to gently sloping roofs with oversized eaves. Floor to ceiling glass is used strategically and rooftops can as easily be covered by a living garden as with tar and gravel. Countering the environmental extremes of the Northwest is always a contributing design consideration, but the end result is neither a Tyrolean castle nor New England saltbox. It is instead, a very clever adaptation of Modernist concepts of openness and simplicity to the climatic demands and regional tastes of the Pacific Northwest.

Jim Olson has always thought of himself as an artist. He is also a person who loves building things. As a teenager, he remembers building a combination dog and cat house for his pets. The dog's quarters were below and the cat's house was on the second level with a ramp for access. In college, he was faced with the choice between art and architecture. He chose the latter but never abandoned the former. He started his firm just out of the University of Washington in Seattle, building his first house on land just south and west of Tacoma. It was a simple building, using modest materials and an earth-tone palette, but it was also a bit ahead of its time in its "green" approach to design. The project won some awards and started Olson's long and well-lauded career.

Tom Kundig was born in California of immigrant parents. His family moved to the Northwest and he grew up in the high desert of eastern Washington and western Idaho, spending his formative years, as have many Northwesterners, exploring the outdoors through activities such as mountaineering and rock climbing. As a young student at the University of Washington, he decided to study physics and geophysics. It wasn't until Kundig started doing some soul searching, however, that he realized he wasn't in the right field. Architecture, his father's profession, was a better fit. He switched majors and completed both of his professional degrees there in 1981. During his summer vacations he worked in the sawmills of the Pacific Northwest, learning firsthand how trees became lumber. He started his professional life working for a mix of Northwest firms before landing a job in Jim Olson's office in 1986. Kundig's technical bent was a good counterpoint to Olson's artistic one. He became a partner in 1994 and the firm took the name Olson Kundig.

Today, Olson Kundig is a large regional architectural firm with projects scattered around the globe. But it has not forgotten its simple roots in residential design which still make up over half of the firm's work. Olson's artistic sensibilities paired with Kundig's mechanical genius have resulted in a distinctive regional architecture that both celebrates the physical beauty of the Northwest and lives compatibly with its environment. Kundig says of his work, "Perhaps because of my upbringing, I have more of an elemental feel for material and details." Olson, on the other hand, is a bit more inspirational and has a pan-aesthetic view of their work. "I see our environment as continuous and connected; everything affects everything else. Architecture should fit into its context in a way that makes a better whole. Climate, culture, landscape or cityscape, architecture, interiors, art ... they are all one integrated environment." One could simply say that Olson has summed up the essence of Rural Modern in three sentences.

Glass Farmhouse

The owners, inspired by Philip Johnson's Glass House, wanted a refuge that opened up to the prairie and mountains of the high-altitude, arid plateau of Eastern Oregon. The buildings Olson designed are conveniently close to each other and enjoy a sense of isolation at the end of a long country road. The roof of the wood-frame barn, which houses farm equipment below and guest rooms above, was inspired by the local vernacular and is echoed in the shed room of the glass house. Olson gave three sides of the house high-efficiency glass window walls framed in steel, with the north wall being a solid exterior. Inside the transparent shell, living, eating, and sleeping areas surround an enclosure that contains the bathroom, study, and storage. The house rests on a concrete slab supported on a concrete foundation. In this way, the heat-absorbing and -releasing thermal mass is isolated from the ground plane. The window system combines transparency with energy-efficiency. Heat loss and gain is managed largely by the orientation of the house: on the south side, an eyebrow, or light shelf, deflects midday summer sun but admits low-angle winter sunlight adding to the house's passive solar design.

Photography by Tim Bies of Olson Kundig

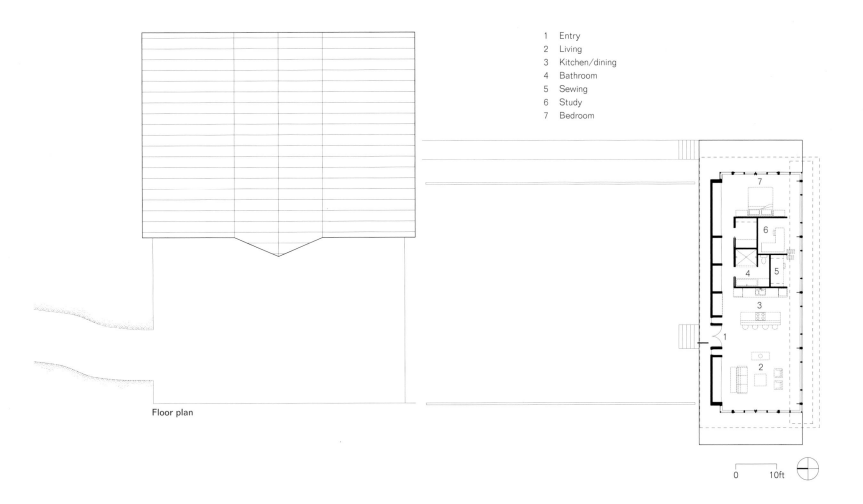

1   Entry
2   Living
3   Kitchen/dining
4   Bathroom
5   Sewing
6   Study
7   Bedroom

Floor plan

0   10ft

A Blend of East and West

Peter Duxbury

Like many Californians, Peter Duxbury is only too happy to admit that he is a transplant to the sunnier environs of the Santa Clara Valley, often called Silicon Valley. He was born, raised, and educated in New York and Connecticut. His family traces its lineage back to the very first European settlers in Massachusetts, but there is little that is conservative in his design approach. While being a natural eclectic, his

"he sees his architecture as a natural growth from the requirements of the site, the environment, and the client's wishes."

work is full of a robust Modernism that California's climate, terrain, and lifestyle afford and encourage. Since opening his practice in 1985, he has maintained a steady flow of clients from the technology world who have asked him to either recreate a house that they dreamed of as children or take them down some less well-charted Modernist path. Fortunately for Duxbury, he is able to do both. From New England cottages to pitched roof Modern, Duxbury's designs cover a lot of stylistic territory, but he is most comfortable designing houses for California's mountainous coastal terrain and he allows the site and the natural environment to be the determining factors in his designs. A believer in passive environmental controls, the architectural features of his houses, such as deep eaves, function as summer sunshades as well as shed winter rains. He insists that he has no architectural heroes and does not consciously try to imitate any style. Instead, he sees his architecture as a natural growth from the requirements of the site, the environment, and the client's wishes. The end result is architecture that is well tailored, thoughtful, and always unpredictable.

Duxbury was born in New York City where his father practiced dentistry. The family moved to Greenwich, Connecticut, an upscale suburb where he grew up. Duxbury jokes that his grandfather was a "patron of the arts" for many years because many of his patients were poor artists who paid him with their work rather than cash. He says their house was filled with hundreds of paintings, sketches and sculptures of his grandfather's patients. They must have been an inspiration for Duxbury who, at a young age, picked up a paintbrush and started painting himself. He went to Syracuse University in New York and earned a professional degree in architecture. Rather than returning to the big city, he joined a firm in Rochester, New York to begin his practice. At the time, the United States was in the middle of a major recession. Having any job in the field was a feat. He was given key responsibilities and several of his projects were built when he was only a few years out of school. His firm was completing a major high-rise project in Rochester and they needed someone to do the tenant interiors. Duxbury was selected and his career took a new path.

Duxbury grew tired of life in the "snow belt" of upstate New York. He had a brother who lived in San Francisco and thought it might be a good career change to come to California. Upon arriving in San Francisco, he quickly landed a job with Gensler who, at the time, was a growing office interior firm that was branching out into other work. Duxbury was a project manager for the interiors of Levi's Corporate Headquarters in San Francisco and was put in charge of a number of large-scale restoration projects on San Francisco's historic waterfront. Gensler asked Duxbury to work with their new Silicon Valley clients and put him in charge of a large corporate project. In 1987, two years after starting his own firm, the CEO of one of the Silicon Valley companies asked Duxbury to design his personal residence. After years of doing corporate work and office planning, he soon found himself working on the residential side of the design business and enjoying it. In 1992 he moved his office from San Francisco to Silicon Valley to be closer to his new residential clients.

Since the early 1990s, Duxbury's small firm has worked with a broad variety of Silicon Valley's citizens, both famous and not. He has developed a distinctive, if not eclectic, practice delivering to his clients a high level design that matches New England pragmatism with California exuberance. He says he likes working in California because the climate and terrain offer both design challenges and freedom not possible in other parts of the country. He prefers doing Modern houses because they so easily fit into the California landscape, but does not always have the opportunity. Duxbury says he goes into each design with no preconceived stylistic approach. He insists that he was a "green" architect before the term was coined. His approach to dealing with the environmental controls is both active and passive, using physical features such as window placement and eaves to control lighting and heat gain as well as geothermal and PV arrays. Like many West Coast architects, he works from the clients' wishes, the constraints of site, and the budget, letting the house design emerge organically. The end result is a more freeform kind of architecture that suits the informal West Coast lifestyle well and is distinctively Californian.

A House in the Santa Lucia Wilderness

This house was built for a professional couple who owned a large parcel in the Santa Lucia Preserve, about two hours south of San Francisco. This area is very rural and was only recently opened up to development. As part of the development agreement, the houses were to be sited on large parcels and conform to strict zoning restrictions and square footage requirements. Duxbury had built two other projects for this client and was the natural choice as their architect.

Duxbury's plan carves into the upslope side of the site and places the garage into the hillside. He then continues the serpentine stone retaining wall to the back side of the house to form an enclosed outdoor living space he calls "the grotto." The main house then steps down the hillside, capturing the spectacular valley and ocean views.

Duxbury organized the house into three sections: a public living section, a home office/work section, and guest quarters for visiting family. When not in use, each section of the house is separated from the other, saving heating and cooling energy. Duxbury says that he designed the house so that it could be lived in as a one-bedroom apartment or a grand gathering space for a large family reunion. The house uses a geothermal heating and cooling system and has a large PV array on the roof that is mostly concealed.

Sitting snuggly into the contours of the rolling hills above the Pacific coastline, Duxbury's Santa Lucia house makes a strong statement for ecological design in a spectacularly beautiful place.

Photography by Russell Abraham

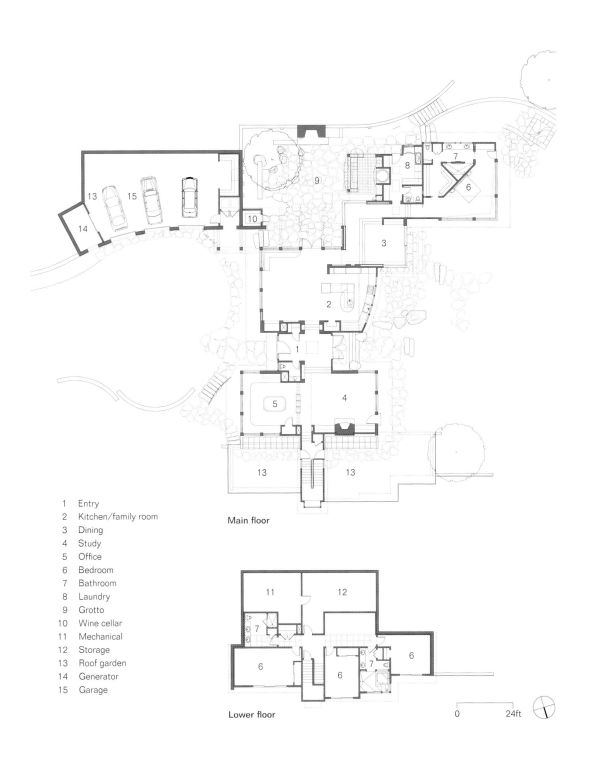

1   Entry
2   Kitchen/family room
3   Dining
4   Study
5   Office
6   Bedroom
7   Bathroom
8   Laundry
9   Grotto
10 Wine cellar
11 Mechanical
12 Storage
13 Roof garden
14 Generator
15 Garage

Main floor

Lower floor

0   24ft

Pacific Northwest Native Son

Geoff Prentiss

The Pacific Northwest of the United States is one of the country's more unusual physical environments. Its geology, a creation of colliding tectonic plates, presents a dramatic plateau of forested mountains that meet a sometimes wild and angry ocean. It also happens to be one of the wettest places in North America with rainfall that can be measured in feet instead of inches. The dynamic and urbane city of Seattle sits on the shores of Puget Sound, a large bay with dozens of inhabited islands whose primary contact with the mainland is through a sophisticated network of sea-going ferries. The economy of the region has shifted

> *"It is a robust regional Modernism that is tailored to accommodate the local climate and make use of readily available regional materials and building tropes."*

in recent decades from primary industries of lumber production and fishing to high tech and aerospace manufacturing, making Seattle one of the more prosperous and livable cities in the United States. It is here that Geoff Prentiss practices his trade.

Prentiss is an amazingly prolific architect in a region known for its distinctive architecture and good local architects. His practice, by design, is primarily residential. Prentiss says that he likes the personal nature of doing residential work. His architecture is uniformly of the Modernist camp, but contains elements of Asian design and a craftsman-influenced Northwest style that gives it a uniqueness and intrigue. Many of his houses are second homes built in the idyllic San Juan Islands just north of Seattle in the Puget Sound. It is here that mild summers with long days are met with blustery rain-soaked falls and winters. Prentiss' houses are designed to take advantage of both. He knows the area well. His ancestors were among its earliest

European settlers in the 19th century. His personal cabin is on land that was bought by his grandfather in 1918 and has remained in his family ever since. "History as place is important to me. Space that makes place is important to me. When you can add history into it to make space, that is wonderful," says Prentiss. All this being said, his architecture is anything but historical eclecticism. It is a robust regional Modernism that is tailored to accommodate the local climate and make use of readily available regional materials and building tropes.

Prentiss grew up in the San Juan Islands of Washington State. His family had lived there for generations. He says he always wanted to be an architect. He also had a strong interest in botany, but architecture held sway. He went to Washington University in St. Louis where he earned a degree in architecture and then went travelling in Latin America for a few years. When he returned to the U.S., he started a landscape design-build business on San Juan Island, his old stomping grounds. While living and working there, he built his first house by himself, acting as architect and contractor. He returned to St. Louis to work on his professional architectural degree, but after one year, he decided to return to Seattle to finish his degree. In 1984 he received a Mombusho Architectural Fellowship to study in Japan where he did research on the interface between interiors and exteriors in traditional and contemporary architecture. He relates that it was a transformational experience; one that informs his work to this day. While going back and forth between Japan and the U.S., he built another vacation home on the San Juan Islands, attracting media attention and winning some awards. He says that when he returned from Japan, he found a ready clientele that has been there ever since.

Prentiss describes himself as a regionalist even though he has done projects as far afield as New York State and Mexico. Even there, "it is strongly important to make a place fit in where it is," he says. If he gets a commission in New York, he wants to try to understand their local building traditions and environmental requirements before he puts pencil to paper. What works in Seattle does not necessarily work in other regions of the country. When asked about the subtle Japanese influence in his work, he emphatically states that it is not conscious, but many people have pointed out that characteristic. He says that he has always appreciated Asian design sensibilities even before he studied there.

The architecture of Geoff Prentiss is uniquely Northwestern, but universal at the same time. His houses have a quiet appeal that could grace many a rural locale, regardless of geography. They are a graceful balance of Modernism, materiality, and regional sensibilities.

North Bay House

The owners of this vacation home desired an intimate, yet dynamic family residence that reflected the beauty of the site and the lifestyle of the San Juan Islands in Puget Sound. Prentiss designed the house to be both a place to gather for large dinners with friends and family as well as a cozy home for the couple when they were alone.

The house is located on a stunning yet restricted site, overlooking Griffin Bay on San Juan Island. The most practical area to build was exactly where three beautiful old-growth trees had already chosen to live. In a prior design, another architect had proposed chopping them down and building right in the middle of the site. Prentiss decided that the trees were an important essence of the site and respectfully had to be preserved. As a result, Prentiss squeezed the programmatic requirements, kept the clients on a square foot restriction and pressed tight against property setbacks. Another design problem was the site's close proximity to the county road, requiring a design that established visual and audio privacy from the road.

Prentiss' design concept was to create a stone wall that swept from the parking to the entry, through the house and out the other side, terminating in a hook that nestled the master shower. This wall became the symbolic and functional shield between the public road and the private living spaces of the home. All the main living spaces and the master suite faced the water, with the remaining rooms tucked into the hill on the road side of the wall.

Offsetting the solid massing of the stone walls, Prentiss created a pavilion which grabs the views and the light to the south, east, and west. Built in a position to be hammered by the winter storms, the pavilion, while light and airy in appearance and feeling, is constructed of glass, steel, stout wood beams, reinforced doors, a stone roof, and a slate floor. The glass pavilion is anchored by two concrete panel chimneys; the windows are steel framed and the exterior skin is of powder coated steel sheathing.

The North Bay House is one more example of good design conquering a difficult site with an innovative solution.

Photography by Jay Goodrich

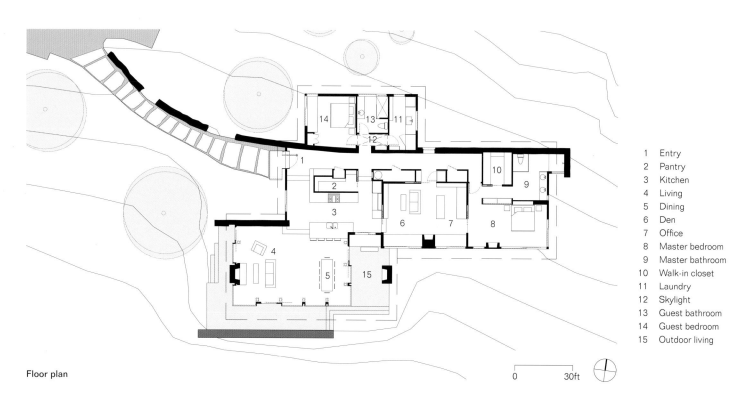

Floor plan

1   Entry
2   Pantry
3   Kitchen
4   Living
5   Dining
6   Den
7   Office
8   Master bedroom
9   Master bathroom
10 Walk-in closet
11 Laundry
12 Skylight
13 Guest bathroom
14 Guest bedroom
15 Outdoor living

0   30ft

Making the Old New

Robert Cain

Robert Cain's career has been as varied and wide-ranging as his work. He is a native son of the Deep South, born, raised, and educated in Alabama, but has practiced all over the United States,

"Using southern yellow and long leaf heart pine, structural steel, and plate glass, he creates houses that are warm, aesthetically edgy, and inviting at the same time."

from Boston to San Francisco. He is a contemporary and former schoolmate of D. K. Ruth and Samuel Mockbee, who started the Rural Studio at Auburn University shortly after Cain began private practice. Cain has practiced in Atlanta for the last 24 years and his work has been a mix of institutional, commercial, and residential design with a healthy mix of adaptive rehab. He has received significant recognition for all of his work but especially for his striking residential work, which is, simply put, vernacular Modern. His houses are full of historical Southern design tropes, but quite modern in both their appearance and function. Using southern yellow and long leaf heart pine, structural steel, and plate glass, he creates houses that are warm, aesthetically edgy, and inviting at the same time. His houses have a distinctive Southern regional quality while being thoroughly Modern. Their steep gabled roofs and wide porches are strongly reminiscent of the rural Southern landscape. Yet Cain reworks these traditional forms and creates something totally Modern.

With his father an engineer, Cain found himself involved in architecture from an early age. He attended Auburn University, where he was exposed to an architecture program that offered a more hands-on approach to architecture. Cain speaks affectionately of his education at Auburn where they took a comprehensive approach to architecture, incorporating both the design and building aspects. In college, he liked the idea that his drawings and sketches were strong enough to speak for themselves. Shortly after college, Cain landed a job with a large North Carolina firm where he went from junior draftsman to Chief Designer over a 10-year period. He says he then decided to hit the road, hiring himself out as a freelance architectural designer in cities around the country. He went from Charlotte, to San Francisco, Santa Fe, Phoenix, and finally Boston where he decided to return to the South and set up a firm with a few acquaintances. His association with the firm didn't last, but Cain's tenure in Atlanta did.

Since his return to the South, Cain has developed a small but vital practice that has residential work at its core. He says he enjoys working with old buildings and either renovating them for their original use, such as old Victorians, or repurposing them such as abandoned industrial buildings. His new residential work is and innovative mix of vernacular themes and Modernism. Some of his Modern houses make extensive use of recycled woods harvested from old buildings. He often designs both furniture and casework from these recycled materials. He recently purchased an old mill town just outside of Atlanta with the intent of renovating it into a small village for creative types.

By borrowing from the old to create the new, Robert Cain represents a progressive force in the architecture of the New South. His work makes a powerful statement for regionalism in a region steeped in its own history and culture.

Brair Creek House

The Briar Creek house is situated on an old farm on South Carolina's coastal plain. The 300-acre (121-hectare) site may have been a 19th-century plantation but most recently it was used as a farm and a hunting preserve. One of the primary objectives of the homeowner was to create a house that naturally shielded its occupants from the region's long hot summers. The property had a large open field that was bounded by mature stands of live oaks and slash pines forming a natural, north–south view corridor for a future residence. The owners wanted a simple, modern house, but one that respected its vernacular rural setting.

Cain decided to take the popular Southern "shotgun house" design and rework it. By extending gables and eaves to control heat gain from windows and placing them symmetrically on either side of each structure, Cain took maximum advantage of natural cooling. He staggered three narrow "shotgun" forms to maximize views and then connected them with transparent bridges. In the main pavilion, he created a great room that contained all the house's public functions. The ancillary wings were used for sleeping quarters. The great room has a high open-gabled ceiling, ideal for catching summer heat and keeping the lower portions of the room several degrees cooler. The floors, walls, and ceilings are lined in native heart pine while all the casework and some of the furniture are made from native woods that were harvested on site. The exquisite floating dining room table that is the centerpiece of the great room was designed by Cain and fabricated from local heart pine.

Briar Creek House is a striking example of Southern simplicity and modern design.

Photography by Rob Karosis

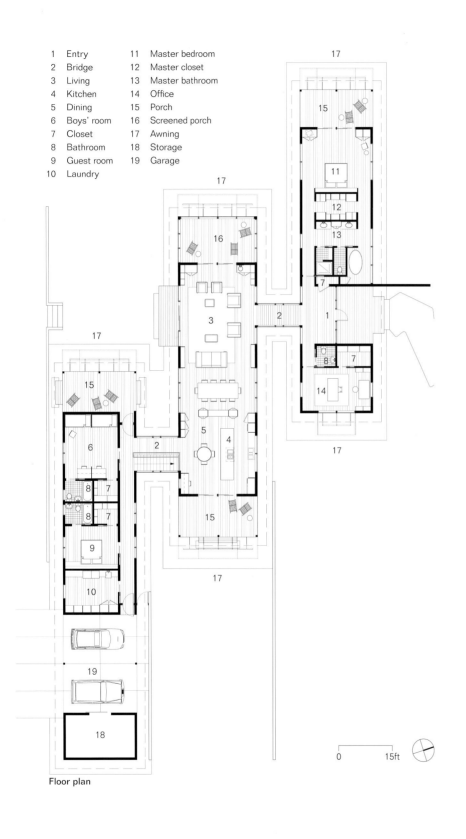

1	Entry	11	Master bedroom
2	Bridge	12	Master closet
3	Living	13	Master bathroom
4	Kitchen	14	Office
5	Dining	15	Porch
6	Boys' room	16	Screened porch
7	Closet	17	Awning
8	Bathroom	18	Storage
9	Guest room	19	Garage
10	Laundry		

0   15ft

Floor plan

California Modernist

Robert Swatt

Robert Swatt calls the San Francisco Bay Area home and has lived there most of his professional life, but he was born and raised on the west side of Los Angeles, and his design sensibilities are informed by a Southern California perspective. With its strong horizontal elements, broad expanses of glass, and easy indoor–outdoor access, his architecture has the look of classic Mid-Century Modern that has gained popularity in the United States and the rest of the world in the last decade. One aspect of his work that separates him from other California Modernists is his liberal

> *"Swatt says he doesn't want his houses to be museums— places you visit and then leave. He wants them to be places that you go to and never want to leave."*

use of natural materials alongside manufactured ones in his design palette. The Cubist forms found in most of his houses are wrapped in dark woods or accented with stone or cement plaster offsetting exposed concrete or steel and walls of glass. It is the simple, yet effective juxtaposition of manufactured and natural materials and the integration of indoor and outdoor spaces that gives Swatt's houses their appeal. Over the last 15 years Robert Swatt's work has received worldwide recognition and he has established his practice as one of the leading Modernist architectural firms in California. His houses skate a thin line between utility and large-scale sculpture. On the other hand, Swatt says he doesn't want his houses to be museums—places you visit and then leave. He wants them to be places that you go to and never want to leave.

Swatt grew up in Los Angeles in the 1950s and 1960s, a period of rapid growth and development in this dynamic urban center. He was surrounded by important monuments to Mid-Century Modernism even though he wasn't aware at the time that his junior high school was designed by Richard Neutra and his grandmother's modest womenswear shop in Hollywood was one of Rudolph Schindler's first commercial projects. Modernism was not only the popular style of the era; it was

part of his heritage. Inspired by an artistic and sensitive extended family, Swatt enrolled in the architecture program at the University of California at Berkeley. It was here that he became exposed to some of the great architectural minds of the day. As a student, he approached Ray Kappe, the influential Los Angeles architect, for a summer job. This initial contact started a lifelong friendship that has lasted to this day. After school, Swatt returned to Los Angeles and landed a job with Cesar Pelli. He says every young architect in the office spent most of their energy trying to shrink the metal mullions of the glass window walls in the buildings they were designing. On the other hand, Swatt was more interested in absorbing the undiscovered Modernist architectural heritage of his native Los Angeles. He spent his evenings and weekends walking the hills of Hollywood and West Los Angeles looking for the hidden architectural treasures of Neutra, Schindler, and Gill.

With his wife and young daughter, Swatt migrated back to Northern California where he opened up his own practice with Bernard Stein. He met early success in his design for hillside homes in the East Bay hills behind Oakland and Berkeley and won several awards, but was soon overtaken by the Post-Modern craze that dominated architectural thinking in the early 1970s and 1980s. In 1995 Swatt bought some property in the rolling hills east of San Francisco and designed a house for himself and his young family, which became a watershed project for his career. Eschewing any Post-Modern artifice, Swatt created a dramatic, Californian Modern house with a marvelous sense of transparency that would rival Schindler. The house won numerous national design awards and established Swatt as a serious proponent of Californian Modernism.

Swatt's firm has grown and expanded ever since. In 2009, he merged with another practice, George Miers Associates, whose focus was on civic, educational, and domestic animal care facilities. Even though his firm today is much larger and more diverse than it was in the mid-1990s,

Swatt still finds his greatest pleasure in designing unique Modernist single family houses, whether they are in gritty urban surrounds or pristine rural settings. His practice is expanding beyond the U.S. borders to projects in Asia and the Middle East.

Today Swatt's architecture is a very pleasing blend of Southern Californian desires and Northern Californian sensibilities. He says, "In L.A. you are more likely to find a client who wants you to do something that has never been done. In the San Francisco Bay Area, you are most likely to find a client who says make it look like the house next door." Swatt's houses manage to skillfully navigate between these two seemingly opposing points of view. Exploiting coastal California's exceptionally mild year-round climate, his houses create drama and excitement with volumetric changes and sweep away window walls that open onto mountain vistas or enchanting courtyards. Tying the house to the land is always the primary design criterion. From there, the subconscious antecedents of Wright and Neutra work their way through the design, giving it a 20th-century grounding with a 21st-century update. Swatt's Cubist forms have a definite Bauhaus ring, while the long, cantilevered overhangs and sunshades are pure Wright. The end result is a California regionalism that is a careful blend of Europe and America. The architecture of Robert Swatt continues a tradition of regional American Modernism that has a unique Californian face.

Stein House

The homeowners of this house were a professional couple with teenage children who owned a merchant-built house in a semi-rural community just east of San Francisco. They loved the spectacular location, but were unhappy with the house's pedestrian and unfunctional plan. They came to Swatt with the hope of rebuilding the house to meet their needs and take full advantage of the site's magnificent hillside location. With the challenge to make the project cost-effective and sustainable, they asked Swatt to reuse whatever he could of the existing property. Swatt's solution was to rebuild the house using the existing foundation—in doing so he saved 20 percent of the rebuilding costs. The new structure reused the existing vehicular approach and orientation but completely reworked the design, allowing for much greater indoor–outdoor access. Swatt's entry solution created a landscaped path along the north side of the house that terminated in a large stucco trellis over a small water feature that led to the oversized front door. Through the door, one entered a great hall with an expansive view of a poolside patio and rolling hills beyond. The main hall faced south and connected two separate wings of the house, both with strong southern views. Because of California's mild coastal climate, the foldaway fenestration on the south side of the house can be opened during the day for most of the year, providing seamless indoor–outdoor access.

The house's strong horizontal overhangs and oversized stucco trellises give it a bit of a Wrightian look and strongly suggest a Mid-Century feel. Swatt denies this was his intent, but the end result is a dramatic house with character that would warm the heart of any Mid-Century aficionado.

Photography by Russell Abraham

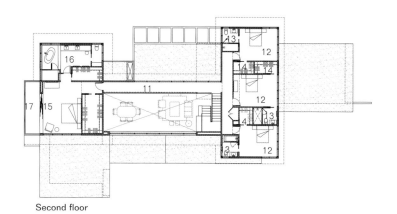

Second floor

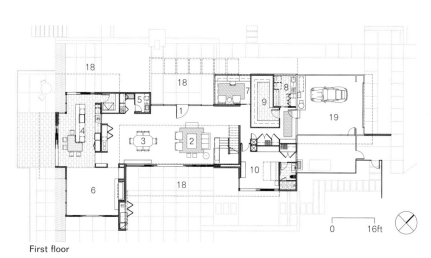

First floor

0　　　　16ft

1	Entry	11	Bridge
2	Living	12	Bedroom
3	Dining	13	Bathroom
4	Kitchen	14	Closet
5	Powder room	15	Master bedroom
6	Family	16	Master bathroom
7	Study	17	Deck
8	Laundry	18	Patio
9	Wine storage	19	Garage
10	Guest bedroom		

An Uncommon Man

Steven Shortridge

It is hard to put a label on Steven Shortridge. His work is clearly Modernist, but no two projects look alike. Each house he designs has a uniqueness that redefines Modernism, whether it be a Cubist beach house in Los Angeles or a deconstructed plantation-style house on Florida's Gulf Coast. Every one of his buildings is designed

"For Shortridge, each project is a clean slate with no 'out of the can' solution or aesthetic."

to fit into its environment and work with existing design themes in a complementary way. Working out of a loft on the west side of Los Angeles, he is surrounded by good examples of Mid-Century Modern architecture. But he is a much more flexible and nuanced architect than many of his fellow Modernist practitioners. Houses he has designed in Europe and the eastern United States all have a regional character that is woven into a Modernist concept. For Shortridge, each project is a clean slate with no "out of the can" solution or aesthetic.

Shortridge was raised in Kentucky and earned his first architectural degree from Texas A&M University. His father was an engineer who built their first house when Shortridge was five. From that point on, architecture was his destiny. He worked for a mid-sized firm in Dallas, Texas before going to MIT in Cambridge, Massachusetts to earn his master's degree. At the time, Maurice K. Smith, the department chair, espoused a philosophy of an organic, regionalist architecture in much the same vein as Wright did a generation earlier. After graduation, Shortridge was faced with the dilemma of deciding where to

practice—New York or Los Angeles. He chose Los Angeles and did not look back. Once there he was offered a position in Frank Israel's office. Israel was a set designer who ventured into architecture and developed one of the most creative practices in Southern California in the early 1990s. Israel died prematurely in 1996, at which point Barbara Callas and Shortridge took over the firm. They continued to function as Callas Shortridge Architects until 2010 when they dissolved the partnership and set up their separate practices.

Today, Shortridge continues to design innovative, Modernist, and Regionalist projects for both residential and commercial clients. His small office in Santa Monica, California produces some of the most interesting and innovative work in the region. He says that the shape of his buildings is as much determined by the eccentricities of his clients and the site than any overarching design concept. Shortridge is the type of architect who thinks in 3D, not 2D. His buildings are not extrusions of floor plans, but a remarkable interplay of three-dimensional spaces. One house he designed on a very tight lot in Venice Beach, California contained seven levels wrapped around a vertiginous central staircase and compacted into a three-story building. His often gray exteriors and hidden entries give way to interior spaces that open up onto verdant hidden courtyards or Piranesian spaces that seem to wind vertically into infinity. Steven Shortridge is a "think outside the box" architect with an effervescent regionalist flair that makes him the uncommon man.

Seagrove House

Designed as a second home for his parents, Shortridge drew heavily from Southern and Gulf Coast design themes to create this dramatic Florida lakefront home. Using a utility pole structural system, he took the highest point on the lakefront and stretched his house to four stories, with most of the living happening on floors one and two. The house sits on Eastern Lake in the Florida Panhandle and is very close to the Gulf of Mexico with its tendency for stormy weather and the occasional tropical storm or hurricane. The house's utility pole system of columns is anchored in a massive concrete foundation, which also serves as the ground floor. Shortridge oriented the house so that each room would have an unobstructed view of the Gulf, just a few hundred yards away. On the top floor, Shortridge placed a screen porch with a corrugated metal roof to allow outdoor living on hot and muggy nights in Florida's Panhandle.

Photography by Richard Sexton

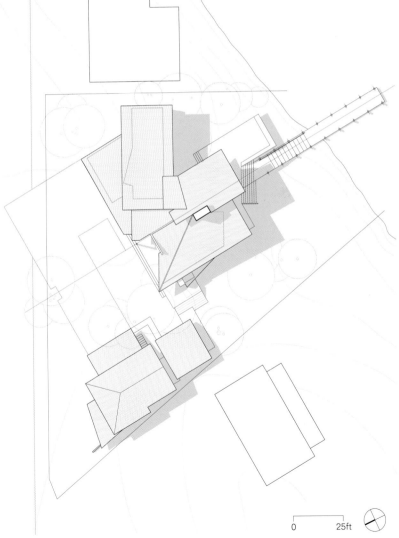

0   25ft

North Carolina's Design Build Architects
Studio B Architecture

Erik Mehlman is a broad-chested man with casual dress and an open demeanor more suited to a builder than an architect. Randy Lanou, the other half of the design-build team, explains the benefits of spatial adjacencies, site orientation, and passive solar strategies more like an architect than a builder. In fact they are both. Mehlman and Lanou own and operate sister companies BuildSense and Studio B Architecture (BS|SBA) in Durham, North Carolina. Together, they offer a full scope of architecture and contracting services to deliver projects from design inception through construction completion. They collaborate on design and construction in their LEED Platinum office

"They believe there is a synergy between the two fields that enhances the design and building processes and yields a better building."

recently completed by BuildSense|Studio B. They refer to the process as "design make design" where one side of the building equation directly influences the other. They believe there is a synergy between the two fields that enhances the design and building processes and yields a better building. Mehlman believes the design-build process can "push the envelope of what can be built." While they have only practiced together for six years, they have won numerous local and regional design awards and attracted attention outside of their central North Carolina region. BS|SBA buildings are simple, smartly designed, and a remarkable blend of modern design and regional contextualism.

Mehlman was born and raised in Rhode Island. At age seven, his family's house burned to the ground and his father hired an architect to design a new home on the existing site. It was at those kitchen table meetings with his father and the architect that Mehlman got an early first-hand introduction to the profession. He went to Tufts University and majored in English while spending summers working in construction and historic restoration. After school he worked briefly in television, at which point he decided he needed a career change. He took classes at the Boston Architectural Center to become familiar with the rigors of the architectural academic environment. Pursuing graduate work at the School of Design at North Carolina State University, Mehlman stayed in North Carolina, earned his license, and set up his practice. In his third year at NC State, he spent a year abroad at the University of the Basque Country in San Sebastian, Spain. For him, that immersion in Spanish culture was likely more valuable an education than were the required studio classes. Mehlman began his professional career working primarily on developer-driven commercial and large-scale multi-family projects in both small and large architectural firms. Mehlman painfully admits that sometimes design was forced to take a back seat under the direction of many bottom line-driven clients. He says, "I did not spend all those years of study and labor to make negative contributions to the built environment." Mehlman decided to pursue smaller, energy-efficient, residential projects where he could have much greater hands-on involvement.

Randy Lanou always liked to make things. He was raised in Santa Cruz, California where he was working on construction sites from a very young age. His parents were serial remodelers so the family home was in a constant state of change. One of the many changes to their home was the creation of a passive solar double-envelope space—Lanou's first introduction to "green" building. Lanou insists on clarifying the "green" of green building with the comment "new term, old idea;" a clue to the fact that he has been committed to environmentally responsible design before its recent popularity. He went on to earn a bachelor's degree in industrial design and worked with a family design-build

company in Illinois. A little later in life, he went back to school to earn a master's degree in architecture at NC State. In 1999, after a few years working in a conventional architecture office, Lanou founded BuildSense, a design-build company focused on building the right way, building with regard to environmental impact, "buildings that make sense."

Mehlman and Lanou met on their first day of classes at NC State. They spent the better part of the next four years working together on school projects, personal projects, or running the School of Design Shop. They kept in touch following graduation and at times discussed the possibility of working together. In 2007, they formed a joint venture, adding an architectural design studio to work with the existing construction firm, using two names, BuildSense and Studio B Architecture. Together, their vision is to "transform American building and foster sustainable living." They focus on green residential design, which has become approximately 85 percent of their business. But their work is more than "eco-friendly." It is strong, modern architecture with a distinctly regional flavor. Passively designing for the environment allows them to use creative solutions and gives their architecture some of its distinctive forms. Deep and broad overhangs tailored to shield the high, hot summer sun yet allow the warmth of winter sun are characteristic of much of their local work. They have a company commitment to "green" certification of their work and their buildings achieve high ratings by both the National Green Building Standard and LEED guidelines. They utilize both high- and low-tech design and devices, but preach conservation before technology. Lanou relates, "It is the boring and unsexy stuff that does the heavy lifting in green design. Start with good framing techniques, insulation, caulking, sealing, flashing, controlled ventilation, material and fixture selections before jumping to solar panels and geothermal." They see their practice as a constant collaboration of design and construction.

Mehlman and Lanou have found the Triangle Area in central North Carolina, with its large, educated populace and an awareness of architecture, a good place to practice. They seem to have found that sweet spot of desirability and affordability in Durham that offers them the opportunity to do creative work for average Americans desiring good design. Simple well-articulated forms blended with hints of regional tastes make their work both accessible and intriguing.

North Carolina's Design Build Architects   199

Spring House

The Spring House was designed by Studio B and built by BuildSense on a previously occupied and heavily wooded lot in the Falls Lake Area of Raleigh, North Carolina. The homeowners wanted a sustainable and energy-efficient home to properly suit the site and "live big" while maintaining a modest appearance. Their two major inspirations included the Japanese exterior veranda and circulation concept of engawa and the style of the "atomic ranch," potentially opposing concepts.

Low sloping roof forms and the massive central stone hearth or entry were the elements of strongest appeal to the owners. The need for multiple stories, the desire for abundant natural daylight, and the owners' request to use alternative materials drove Mehlman to a reinterpretation of classic ranch forms. He transformed the typical heavy masonry element to a delicate and lacy filter of light serving as the entry and vertical circulation core. The perforated aluminum skin he designed defines this "lightbox" to both the exterior and interior while it is an ever-present feature through family gathering spaces. At nightfall it glows like a lantern, becoming a beacon to the exterior and a nightlight to the interior.

The existing home was recycled, diverting over 75 percent of the material from the landfill and allowing for reuse of old framing lumber in the new home including the crafting of a magnificent central stair in the "lightbox."

Spring House is a great example of how "living small" can be "living big."

Photography by Mark Herboth

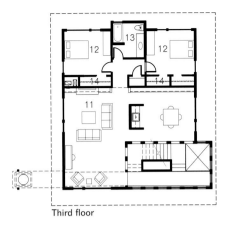

Third floor

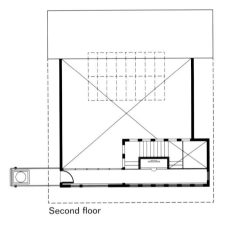

1 Entry
2 Living
3 Dining
4 Kitchen
5 Powder room
6 Master bedroom
7 Master bathroom
8 Walk-in closet
9 Laundry
10 Mudroom
11 Family room
12 Bedroom
13 Bathroom
14 Closet
15 Garage

Second floor

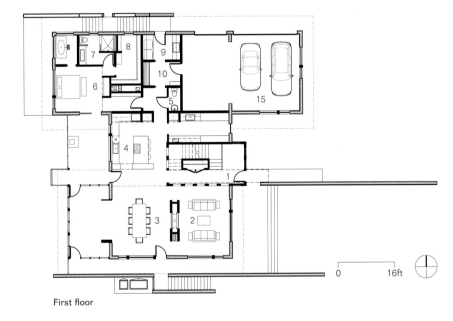

First floor

0   16ft

Seminal Creaters of a Vernacular Style
Turnbull Griffin Haesloop Architects

Mary Griffin, Stefan Hastrup, and Eric Haesloop work out of a bright top floor studio in a rehabbed industrial building just off San Francisco's Van Ness Avenue and not far from downtown. The Turnbull in the

"The firm sees their work as somewhat timeless, but slowly evolving to meet the constraints and innovations of present day building practices and market conditions."

firm's name is William Turnbull. Although he passed away in 1997, his spirit and intellect live on in the work of Turnbull Griffin Haesloop Architects and their many clients, admirers, and acolytes. In the early 1960s, William Turnbull, along with Charles Moore, Donlyn Lyndon, and Richard Whitaker created an innovative architectural style in Northern California that has endured. This architectural style, sometimes know as the Third Bay Tradition or Bay Regional Style, set the bar for residential design for at least a generation. Influenced by both early 20th-century Craftsman-style architects like Maybeck and Mid-Century Modernists like Neutra and Eames, the Third Bay Tradition was a blend of Modernism with the ever-popular Bay Area Shingle Style. Turnbull reached deep into his native California vernacular of rural buildings and married those forms with Modern design and abundant redwood and Douglas fir to create an easily accessible design style that gained instant popularity. Today, Turnbull Griffin Haesloop carries on that cultural tradition of creating arresting architecture with simple materials, vernacular forms, and highly contextual design that blends well into the Northern California landscape.

Both Griffin and Haesloop started life in other parts of the country and only came west at Turnbull's urging. Griffin is a native of Atlanta and grew up in an unusual architect-designed house that was commissioned by her father, a university professor. She never dreamed of being an architect until she ended up in an architecture

history class at Brown University. Later, while working at Harvard, a professor urged her to go to architecture school. While doing graduate work in architecture at MIT, she met Donlyn Lyndon who would become her mentor and would later introduce her to William Turnbull, her future husband. Eric Haesloop grew up in the Midwest, but had family in Germany and would spend his summers there. It was during those summer vacations in Europe that he discovered architecture. He said that as a youth, he didn't have a name for it, but he knew he wanted to be part of it. He did undergraduate work at Washington University with a semester in Salamanca, Spain and then went on to Yale. Upon graduating, he worked for Cesar Pelli for three years, after which he decided that a move to California was on the cards. In short order, he found himself working for Moore, Lyndon, Turnbull, and Whitaker, or more commonly known by the acronym MLTW. Moore, Lyndon, and Whitaker soon left and Turnbull took on Griffin and Haesloop as junior partners.

Stefan Hastrup migrated from Southern California to New England to attend college. Architecture was always in the back of his mind, he says, but he found his undergraduate studies in liberal arts at Brown University useful in broadening his worldview. A summer program in architecture in New York was the professional epiphany he was looking for. He completed the master's program in architecture at Yale University and met Eric Haesloop along the way. Hastrup also took a studio course from Turnbull who was a visiting professor at Yale and their connection was obviously long-lasting. Out of school, Hastrup worked in New York on historic restoration and museum development before he migrated west back to California. He was working for the West Coast office of Polshek and Partners when Haesloop asked him to help out on a small museum proposal they were putting together, and while the proposal didn't win, Hastrup stayed.

The firm has made a conscious decision to remain small and create environmentally-friendly, site-sensitive work with a strong emphasis on sustainable residential design. Haesloop says he doesn't see his work as a style as much as trying to meet the demands of the site. The three principals see their firm as picking up the design process where Turnbull left off. They have a strong appreciation for the vernacular and are very conscious of site-specific design. Haesloop notes how the Sea Ranch Barn, with its lack of overhangs and the way it hugged the land, became the essential design trope for his firm's work and the entire design movement that evolved around it. Griffin says that having the building be attuned to the land and intelligent siting goes a long way toward creating energy-efficient buildings. The firm sees their work as somewhat timeless, but slowly evolving to meet the constraints and innovations of present day building practices and market conditions.

The architects at Turnbull Griffin Haesloop have inherited a significant design heritage from their founder. They see their role as honoring that tradition and at the same time, breathing new life into it for the 21st century.

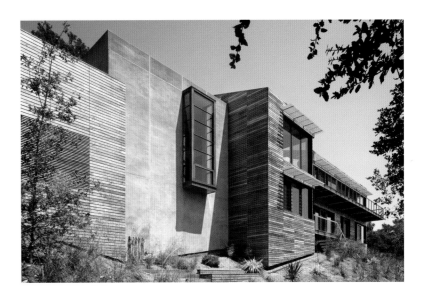

House on a Hill in Marin (Kentfield)

Kentfield is a closed-in suburb in Marin county, but located on the slopes of Mount Tamalpais, it is also hard next to beautiful woodland and open space. The owners of this house were a retired couple who took great pleasure in being an active part of the design process. An existing house on the site was removed and a radical new program developed for it.

Built along a steep hillside, this 5,508-square-foot (511-square-meter) house emerges gracefully from the land and captures the stunning, unobstructed views of Mount Tamalpais and San Francisco Bay. A retaining wall to the north follows the undulating contours of the topography, anchoring and shaping the uphill side of the residence.

The garden rooftop becomes a visual extension of the hillside, discreetly tucking the structure underneath and fusing the residence with the landscape. The living roof collects and filters stormwater runoff, feeding to a 2,500-gallon (9,460-liter) cistern that is used for landscaping and slowly recharges the groundwater.

Three volumes physically define and house the living room, kitchen-dining area, and master bedroom spaces, rising above the living roof with sloped-roofs that are angled to capture the sun for photovoltaic and solar hot water panels. Simple, yet elegant materials express the residence's form, as well as characterize an enduring connection to the environment.

Photography by David Wakely

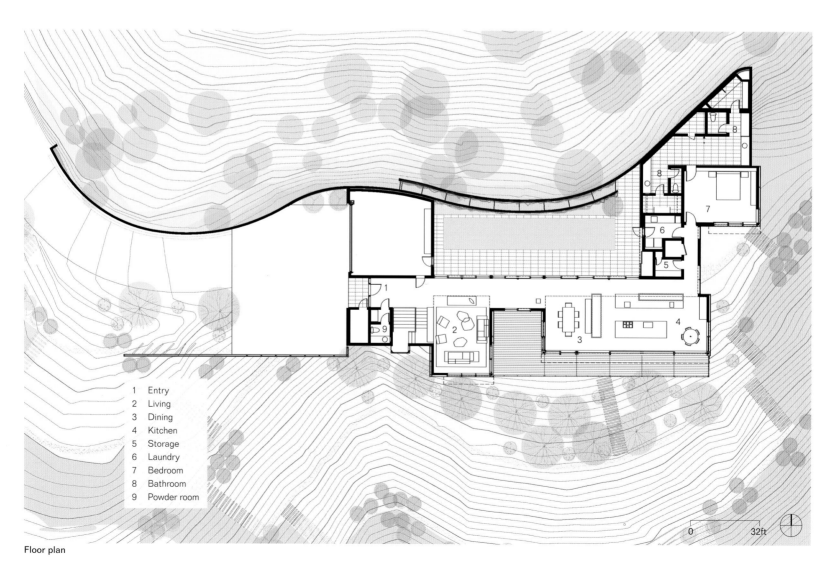

1 Entry
2 Living
3 Dining
4 Kitchen
5 Storage
6 Laundry
7 Bedroom
8 Bathroom
9 Powder room

Floor plan

Contextual Craftsman

W. David Martin

William David Martin is an unusual architect. He works out of California's central coast, a region blessed with a world-famous coastline, a mild climate and spectacular scenery. He designs houses for the rich and famous and those who would like to be, but he also enjoys designing additions and remodels for family and friends. Running an almost micro-office organization, he says that his projects are often drawn up on a client's kitchen table or the trunk of a car. His approach to design

"There is a visual unity that speaks to a West Coast design sense that permeates all of his work."

involves heavy client input that often yields a style of architecture that is eclectic, regional, and very grounded in his California roots. But Martin is no homespun craftsman builder. He is a serious architect with a very deep resume in large-scale international work who has decided to devote his practice to smaller scale commercial and residential work. He jokes that his first major architectural project was an international airport and entire new city in Saudi Arabia and his last will probably be a birdhouse in Carmel. Looking at his work, one can find a little bit of everything from Maybeck and Wright to Neutra and Mies, but there is a visual unity that speaks to a West Coast design sense that permeates all of his work. Even when his clients demand something grand, Martin finds a way to make it intimate and livable.

Martin was born in Coronado, California, a suburb of San Diego and an important center for the United States Navy. His father was a high-ranking naval officer who was given major commands around the world and the family was always moving. Martin says he lived in 23 houses and went to 17 schools, including 4 high schools, when he was growing up. Following his father's footsteps he was admitted to the United States Naval Academy, but because of a sports injury needing immediate surgery, he went to the University of Southern California on a Navy scholarship instead. He majored in engineering, but transferred to

architecture after his first year, graduating with a professional degree and a commission as an officer in the Navy Civil Engineer Corps. The Navy wasted no time putting him to work on numerous building projects around the world. At one point, Martin ended up in Da Nang, Vietnam, as a young Company Commander with a Mobile Construction Battalion in charge of 126 men building facilities for the Marines. While completing his assigned construction projects, Martin adopted seven hamlets of Vietnamese refugees in the Da Nang area and developed a Civic Action program that paired his Seabees with refugees to build over 400 homes, a maternity hospital, and an orphanage, while dodging enemy fire. A clubhouse he designed and built from salvaged materials was published in *Progressive Architecture*. Martin says that working in a war zone, while a very sobering experience, also equipped him with leadership skills and an appreciation of the value of teamwork and shared responsibility in creating livable environments with very limited resources.

After completing his third tour of duty in the Navy, Martin decided to re-enter civilian life and start his architectural career. He was accepted in the graduate program at MIT and graduated with a Master's in Architecture and a second Master's in City Planning. From MIT, Martin began work with the Boston office of Skidmore, Owings & Merrill, doing very large-scale highway and urban design work for that city. In addition to new subway extensions and stations, he was a principal designer for relocating the Central Artery underground in the heart of the city, connecting it to a new harbor tunnel to the airport in East Boston. Martin also found time to teach and be a guest critic at Boston University, MIT, and Harvard.

Martin wanted to return to his native California, but SOM had just landed a huge project in Saudi Arabia and wanted him to be part of it. He moved to Washington, D.C. where he started on the initial planning work for a new International Airport and Royal Saudi Air Force base

near the city of Jeddah. He began commuting between New York and Washington D.C. every week, but when he was asked to move to New York City and work full time on the Saudi project, he decided it was time to move west. On his way back to Southern California he decided to take a long weekend and visit some friends in the central California town of Monterey. At the time, Monterey was transitioning from a fishing and agricultural community to one based on tourism. There were resorts, hotels, restaurants, churches, art galleries, and vacation homes to be built and for the next 15 years Martin enjoyed designing in each of these niches with several local firms. At age 49 he figured it was time to start his own firm with a simple commitment to serve the California central coast by "creating spaces that nurture and inspire."

The Monterey Peninsula is known for its stunning natural beauty. Immortalized by John Steinbeck's novels, it was also known for its sardine fleet and lettuce production, but it has always had some ranking as a resort destination. In the late 19th century, a railway line was built from San Francisco, and a lodge and golf club built for the city's swells. The less fortunate folk vacationed in tent encampments run by religious organizations a few miles away in Pacific Grove. Julia Morgan, the noted early-20th-century San Francisco architect, designed a Girl Scout camp perched on the edge of the Pacific, called Asilomar, whose original buildings still exist and have been converted into an international conference center. Samuel F. B. Morse developed a lush, upscale golf community called Pebble Beach and built it around a golf course right on the Pacific Ocean. To this day, the Pebble Beach Golf Course draws golfers from around the world. In recent years, some of the outlying ranches have been developed as preserves for residential use, with houses occupying very large acreage. It is in these environments that W. David Martin has found his niche as an architect.

Martin's clients are as varied as the people who visit and inhabit the Monterey Peninsula, from simple middle-class homeowners needing a remodel to wealthy finance or computer industry moguls looking for a weekend getaway in "paradise." He tailors his houses to meet his clients' expectations and budgets, but his craftsman like approach and strong sense of Modernity shine through every project.

River View Residence

The clients for this elegant retreat were a professional couple from the San Francisco Bay Area who had owned the property for a number of years and asked Martin to completely rebuild their weekend home. They loved the water views and wanted Martin to preserve much of the natural beauty of the land, but also wanted a house that made something of a Modernist statement. The clients were fans of Mid-Century Modernism that was a popular part of post-war California design.

The program for this house was to capture both the spectacular estuary views and also provide ample indoor–outdoor space relationships preserving their privacy. Martin borrowed his design program from the regional Spanish-themed house. He gave the house a strong sandstone wall that faced the street. In the middle of the imposing wall, he placed oversized double-hung glass and steel entry doors that open into an internal glazed courtyard, which leads through a small garden to the main entry door—a shear wall of glass with a breathtaking view of the estuary beyond. To give a feel of visual continuity and excitement, Martin suspended a serpentine metal sculpture that wends its way from the courtyard, through the living room, and out into the rear patio. The serpentine sculpture's wave form is repeated horizontally in the three roof soffits that face the rear of the house. A lush garden and firepit grace the rear of the house, in stark contrast to the wild greenery of the estuary and coastal mountainside just steps away. Martin designed a cantilevered glass staircase that leads from the family room to a guest bedroom above the garage.

This compact, intricately designed house makes a dramatic statement on the California coast by reworking traditional regional design themes and materials to create something thoroughly Modern.

Photography by Russell Abraham

Loft

1	Atrium	8	Loft
2	Entry	9	Bedroom
3	Living	10	Bathroom
4	Utility	11	Office
5	Family room	12	Dressing room
6	Kitchen	13	Garage
7	Dining		

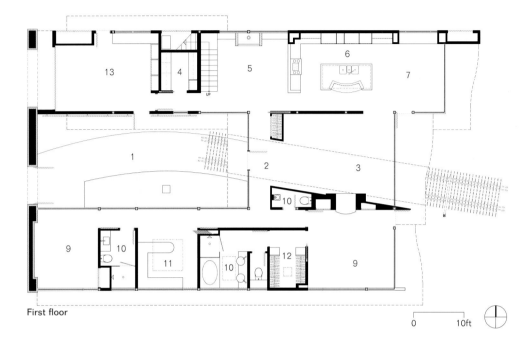

First floor

0   10ft

Living in a Sweet Spot

Walker Warner Architects

Brooks Walker and Greg Warner occupy a sweet spot in the design world. Their clients are fortunate enough to afford to build what they design, without demanding ostentation or crassness. Their practice spreads throughout the West Coast and the Hawaiian Islands and centers itself around a tasteful style they describe as "Warm Modernism" with vernacular references. Talking about their work is like describing a good wine—a bit ironic since designing wineries in the Napa and Sonoma Valleys happens to be one of their firm's specialties. Warner jokingly says that they are fortunate enough to design "unaffordable housing." But their houses are more than pleasure palaces for the wealthy. They are refined, elegant statements about a regional Modernism that is pervasive in California and other

"Using regional materials, combined with a sophisticated compendium of vernacular forms, they create buildings that are both inviting and challenging."

parts of the West Coast. Using regional materials, combined with a sophisticated compendium of vernacular forms, they create buildings that are both inviting and challenging. Warner likes to think of their work as "legacy houses" that will stand up to the test of time and serve generations of owners. Their work may reference the farmhouse on the hill, but quickly leaves that trope and ventures into some uncharted and intriguing design territory that is both tactile and visually exciting.

Greg Warner grew up in Waimea, a ranching town located on the Big Island of Hawaii. He went to a prep school there that was designed by the distinguished Hawaiian architect Vladimir Ossipoff. Each Sunday night he would sit in the school's Modernist, poured-in-place concrete chapel and contemplate the building's awesome power. This left a hidden but lasting impression, one that he would get to revisit later in his career. It was many years later that he would discover the completed works of Ossipoff and gain a full appreciation for his influence on architecture in Hawaii.

At the University of Oregon, he fell into the architecture program almost as an afterthought, hoping it would be a good fit, considering that he enjoyed fine art and drawing and felt architecture might be a good outlet for his creative side. There he met Brooks Walker. They shared classes and were friends, but their later partnership was still to come.

Brooks Walker is a California native son whose family has had a long involvement in progressive architecture. He grew up visiting houses that were designed by Wurster and Wright in the 1930s. His uncle is a well-known San Francisco architect with a sterling list of clients, and appreciation for art and design was part of the family's DNA. It was only natural for Brooks to study architecture. Working from a regionalist perspective, the philosophy at the University of Oregon School of Architecture was to create sustainable buildings with a respect for "place." Walker returned to San Francisco and began work with his uncle. Following an opportunity to design and build a house for his sister, he left that firm. At the same time, Warner was working for a small firm in the Bay Area and was ready to move on. Over a kitchen table powwow the firm was formed—Walker had the work and Warner had a T-square. Walker Warner Architects quickly built a solid reputation as young architects with good taste and sophisticated designs.

Warner says that as the firm has matured, they have become more focused on doing the type of architecture their firm has become known for over the last 20 years. They have been fortunate to find sophisticated clients who have come to them looking for unpretentious, well-thought-out design that pushes the envelope in creative ways. Just recently, while working on a project in Hawaii, Warner visited his old prep school and was reminded why he chose his profession and the tacit influences of his Hawaiian upbringing. Ossipoff's Mid-Century Modern buildings spoke to him in ways he could just now comprehend, simple unpretentious architecture that spoke to both time and place in an elegant way. If only Vladimir Ossipoff could have known that his work inspired the next generation of great architects.

Woodside House

Woodside House is an agrarian enclave located between two urban centers in northern California. The rolling green hills and horse farms look more like Kentucky than California. The owners of this house wanted a modern building that respected the area's rural nature. Warner's concept for this project began as an exploration of separate buildings arranged on the site to create a variety of complementary indoor/outdoor spaces along with varied living experiences. Given the rural context of the town, Warner referenced regional agrarian compounds and barn forms for inspiration as well as functionality.

All of the compound's component buildings share a common language of strong asymmetrical lines and a material palette of stone, wood, glass, and steel to create a balanced feeling throughout. Warner chose stone to evoke rusticity, linking the structures to the past, while the random patterned cedar planks, along with zinc roofing, reference the rural vernacular farm buildings in the region. The inclusion of exposed steel and large expanses of glass give the residence a contrasting, contemporary feel.

The barn, located at the front of the property, serves as a symbolic entry reinforcing the rural character of the surrounding context. An open passageway leading through the barn dramatically frames the stone entry façade of the residence beyond. Upon entering the courtyard, which is loosely formed by the three structures, the intent of the initial concepts is revealed. Building façades complement each other while maintaining independently strong connections to the property and surround.

Photography by Matthew Millman

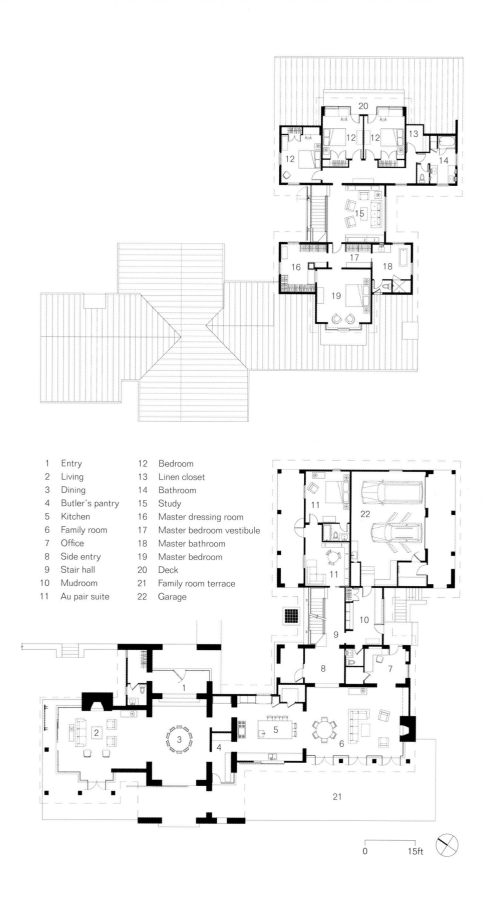

1   Entry
2   Living
3   Dining
4   Butler's pantry
5   Kitchen
6   Family room
7   Office
8   Side entry
9   Stair hall
10 Mudroom
11 Au pair suite
12 Bedroom
13 Linen closet
14 Bathroom
15 Study
16 Master dressing room
17 Master bedroom vestibule
18 Master bathroom
19 Master bedroom
20 Deck
21 Family room terrace
22 Garage

0   15ft

Genius in the Desert

Will Bruder

The Sonoran desert is a livelier and lusher place than its Mohave cousin to the west. Its ridges and washes are dotted with statuesque Saguaro, fragrant creosote, delicate green Mesquite, and Palo Brea. Over 300 species of birds and 60 species of mammals populate its sky

"His buildings create spaces that can be grand, intimate, and challenging at the same time."

and terrain. Its dry and mild fall, winter, and spring are punctuated by a blistering hot summer broken only by end of the day thunderstorms that blow up from Mexico. It is here, in this starkest of environments that some of America's most iconic and revolutionary 20th-century architects have chosen to set up shop and call home: Frank Lloyd Wright, Paolo Soleri, and now Will Bruder. In this natural cauldron, a place "where the Sun kisses the Earth" almost on a daily basis, great architects have found a way to create architecture amidst the desert solitude and suburban sprawl and late-20th-century urban banalities.

Will Bruder did not grow up in Arizona. Like Wright, he is the native son of the upper Midwest of the United States and like Wright, he migrated to the desert to flap his wings and let his creative spirit soar. In a career that has lasted close to 40 years, his fecund creative output has left a significant mark both in the desert and beyond. Almost every one of Bruder's buildings has a sculptural quality that takes them beyond architecture and questions what you can legitimately do with form and materials. One can always find a grand gesture in his work—a rakishly sloping wall or a huge curved surface—but it is in the subtle use of geometry, the clever ordering of spaces, the outlandish but appropriate detailing of unexpected materials that make his work so extraordinary. His buildings create spaces that can be grand, intimate, and challenging at the same time. Working in desert isolation, he has been able to create a vital regional Modernism that has been liberated from Post-

Modern influences so trendy during a significant part of his professional life. His desert vernacular Modern style charts a path into the 21st century that younger architects could only hope to imitate.

Bruder grew up in an inner suburb of Milwaukee, Wisconsin in the post-WWII period. He says he was exposed to the Mid-Century Modernists like Saarinen and Perkins and Will from the recently built schools he attended.

Fifth grade was an epiphany for Bruder. With the strong encouragement of Miss Timm, his fifth grade teacher, Bruder discovered his creative side. About two miles from his home by bicycle, a new Greek Orthodox Church was being built. It was a poured-in-place concrete structure that Bruder "crashed" on a regular basis, crawling under a construction barrier and observing the building process first hand. The church's architect was Frank Lloyd Wright.

Bruder started building model cars that he designed from scratch for the popular national Fisher Body car competition. He built four cars and won awards for all of them. In the process, he was flown to Detroit to meet professional car designers. He remembers walking up the stairs to Saarinen's General Motors Tech Center just outside Detroit and being in awe. Only later did he discover who Saarinen was.

Bruder toyed with the idea of being an industrial designer and applied to the Illinois Institute of Technology, with the idea of becoming an auto designer. A stroke of luck and a family connection led him to a job with William Wenzler, a young, Modernist architect with a thriving practice in Milwaukee. It was here, in Wenzler's office, that he first began his apprenticeship. In order it maintain his position at Wenzler, he transferred to the University of Wisconsin, Milwaukee. At the time, Wisconsin was the only state university in the country that did not have an architectural program. Not to be deterred, Bruder studied every subject necessary to obtain an architecture degree without having

access to a design studio. He graduated with a bachelor of fine arts in Sculpture. Bruder heard about the visionary Paolo Soleri and made the pilgrimage to his studio in Arizona where he was invited to work for five weeks in 1967. It was during this initial internship with Soleri that he was exposed to the Sonoran desert. The summer heat and carefree desert lifestyle left their mark. He returned a year later and stayed for eight months. He says he did everything there, from graphics, to mixing concrete, to pouring bronze. He returned to Wisconsin, finished his degree and then landed a job in Detroit with Gunnar Birkerts, the famous Latvian immigrant Modernist, and a student of Saarinen. He stayed with Birkerts for one year and then decided to return to Arizona. He worked for various firms in Phoenix until he logged enough time to take his licensing exam. He passed on his first try and immediately opened his studio

Recognition came quickly for Bruder. His first house, an inexpensive cabin in Flagstaff, won a National Plywood Association award. In 1977, his own house was selected for inclusion in *Architectural Record*'s *Record Houses* annual. In the mid-1970s his firm started getting public work, which has continued to this day. In 1987, he won the Rome Prize and spent six months at the American Academy in Italy studying and observing ancient and modern architecture. He says his Rome experience "changed his life." Upon returning to Phoenix, he won the opportunity to build the Phoenix Central Library, establishing his design firm on an international stage, fully qualified to create dynamic, large-scale public works.

Once his firm had expanded by three partners, some 30 employees, with major projects across the West and in Saudi Arabia, Bruder decided to step back and return to his roots of a smaller more hands-on studio practice. In an amicable separation, Will Bruder Architects is back to a five-person firm focusing on residential, cultural, and civic work. Bruder, who has always thought of himself as a bit of an "outsider," is once again an outsider by choice.

At a self-described mid-point in his life, Bruder sees years of creativity in front of him. Bruder says "What I learned from Soleri was how to make the ordinary extraordinary. My sculpture background is about scale, about proportion, about detail, about materiality, about light, about shadow. Those are my tools." Bruder has also become a

more urban person, living and working in downtown Phoenix, involved in turning his city into a more people-friendly place. Bruder says that a native regionalism is at the heart of everything he does. He insists that every building he designs "talks about the history of making, the history of place, and the climate." In certain ways he thinks of himself as a curious archeologist when he starts a project in a new location, learning the history of building there.

Will Bruder is the rare architect who can synthesize a lot of ideas to create a building that is grounded, practical, beautiful, and just outside anyone's preconceived notion of what it should look like. His work in Arizona is informed by the blistering summer heat; by the corrugated steel agricultural buildings of the early 20th century; by the Sonoran desert adobes; and by just what the next concept car from Detroit should look like. His curious mind is constantly asking questions and finding innovative design solutions to age-old building problems. Like Wright and Soleri before him, he is an American original whose architectural designs have been tempered in the blast furnace-like heat of the Sonoran desert and succeeded.

Jarson House

Everything about the Jarson House is exceptional—its private and serene desert location with dramatic views, its simple metallic sheathed form that slices like a knife into the desert terrain, its simple yet effective arrangement of spaces, its clever and sophisticated detailing. The elegance of the Jarson House lies more in its simplicity than any grand architectural gesture. Bruder knows the desert and knows that the only way he can get large walls of glass is to face them north, which he does. Bruder knows the south side of the house will be pounded year round by the blistering sun. His solution is to tuck that side into the hill separated by a stone wall made from on site material and a narrow walkway.

In Jarson, Bruder skews geometries so that each space is a trapezoid that opens on the wide side to the views of the valley below. Even though the house is essentially a wood-framed structure, Bruder uses steel, copper, and glass in both decorative and non-conventional ways. The main staircase is trapezoidal with aluminum risers and cork treads. The windows on the south side of the house have oversized steel casings that extend several inches into each space. The north and east sides of the building are sheathed in copper while the south and west sides facing the hill are corrugated weathered steel with a vented backing to shed heat. A large glass window separates the master bath from the main staircase, providing both privacy for the bath and light for the staircase. Tucked away behind the kitchen and art room is a covered breezeway that provides both a shaded outside space and a semi-private space to do crafts.

The Jarson House is essential Will Bruder: elegant, practical, very well thought out, and filled with the unexpected—qualities that separate great architecture from good architecture.

Photography by Russell Abraham

234 Rural Modern

1   Entry
2   Dining
3   Living
4   Kitchen
5   Pantry
6   Powder room
7   Bedroom
8   Bathroom
9   Master bedroom
10   Master bathroom
11   Walk-in closet
12   Deck

Second floor

First floor

0   16ft

Index of Architects

Biography

Russell Abraham is one of the leading architectural photographers and emerging architectural writers in the United States. He has the unique ability both to write about and to photograph architecture in an incisive way. His work has appeared in numerous books and trade journals on architecture and interior design. He has mentored and trained many well-known architectural photographers practicing today. This book is the fifth he has either written or photographed a significant part of and the second that he has created in its entirety.

As young man, Abraham was always interested in the fine arts and design. He migrated west from his native Pennsylvania to attend the University of California, Berkeley, where he earned degrees in architecture and design. Along the way, he found peering through the camera lens more interesting than peering at the drafting table. He started his professional career as a photojournalist, but was drawn back to architecture early on. Over the years, he has worked with many of the West Coast's leading architectural firms and he enjoys being part of the creative process, with an insider's view of architecture.

Abraham lives in the oak-studded, rolling hills just east of San Francisco with his wife, an artist, and one of his four children in a house designed by one of this book's contributors.

Acknowledgements

The concept for this book has been percolating in the back of my mind for several years. Many of the architects I work with in California are Modernists with a regional stamp that is distinctly Rural Modern. I would like to thank architect David S. Wilson who brainstormed with me and came up with a title that just would not go away. He introduced me to architects around the United States whose work fit well under the title's soubriquet. I also would like to thank Kate R. Carboneau who collaborated in researching some great architectural firms in the Southeast and assisting me on a number of the shoots on both coasts. Finally, I would like to thank the publishers of Images Publishing, Alessina Brooks and Paul Latham, for their continued support in bringing my images and ideas to life.

Russell Abraham